The God-Man of Galilee

STUDIES IN CHRISTIAN LIVING

Howard Moody Morgan

Reston Publishing Company, Inc.
A Prentice-Hall Company
Reston, Virginia

Library of Congress Cataloging in Publication Data

Morgan, Howard Moody
  The God-Man of Galilee

  1. Presbyterian Church-Sermons. 2. Sermons,
American. I. Title
BX9178.M596G63 1983 252'.051 83-11065
ISBN 08359-2561-7

© 1983 Morgan Associates, Ltd.

Printed in the United States of America

10 9 8 7 6 5 4 3 2 1

Text prepared and book designed by Robert Scharff
and Associates, Ltd.

CONTENTS

ACKNOWLEDGEMENTS

Permission to review and publish some of Dr. Morgan's sermons was graciously given by his wife, Kax. Each of Dr. Morgan's five children agreed to publication and helped in the process. A special word of appreciation should be given to Howard Campbell Morgan, who was instrumental in arranging for publication. To other members of Dr. Morgan's family—in this country and in England, living and departed—this book is dedicated. Scriptural passages quoted in the sermons are from the King James Version of the Bible.

TO MY FATHER

The pulpit seems bare now, the sanctuary deserted.
There is no need for further exposition.
Above Broad Street the grey steeple
Stretches, crying to the sky.
This day you are no longer here
And I, without a text, must mourn.
And we are children, living within time.
And we are children, looking for a sign.
But what sign would you give to us?
A measured voice, your English lyric?
A father's hand, our essential delight?
I think perhaps the laughing eyes
That saw the joy of every moment.
Now you, who ministered to others,
Must pray for us
Who suffer such a loss.
Somewhere, deep among familiar stars,
I know you hear.
Your gift of words, and of The Word,
You gave them freely,
And lost them in the heat of life.
And we live to speak them, hear them,
Write them, have them, be them.
No living word ever dies
But is transported back to life.
Dear Father, here thy servant keep,
As shepherds gather in their sheep;
Home, home at last, his days are done
And now the final victory won.

(Written by Dr. Morgan's son, John,
and read at his memorial service,
October, 1979.)

INTRODUCTION

"Have A Good Day" was his final sermon. He delivered this sermon in 1979 at a Presbyterian Church in Philadelphia, Pennsylvania, a city with which he had become intimately familiar since assuming a pastorate there in 1933. He chose as his text these words from II Peter, Chapter Three, Verse Eight: "But, beloved, be not ignorant of this one thing, that one day *is* with the Lord as a thousand years, and a thousand years as one day." This scriptural choice was both prophetic and personally character-istic of Howard Moody Morgan, son of the internationally known Biblical expositor, G. Campbell Morgan. If he could have written his own last words, surely they would have contained notes of joy and affirmation. At the bottom of his sermon notes on this last proclamation, one also finds his handwritten summation: "Thou knowest, O Man, what is good, what the Lord requires of thee: To do justly, to love mercy, to walk humbly with thy God."

For over five decades Dr. Howard Moody Morgan was a preacher of the Word and a pastor to his congregation. He served the greater part of his ministry in Philadelphia but journeyed often as a preacher to churches in England.

He received his theological training from his father, who is reported by the *New York Times* as "one of the foremost Bible scholars of his age." He had followed G. Campbell Morgan as pastor of the Tabernacle Presbyterian Church in Philadelphia. On June 15, 1945, a memorial service was held at Tabernacle Church for G. Campbell Morgan. The words of Dr. Charles R. Erdman of Princeton, New Jersey spoken of G. Campbell Morgan might well have applied to Howard Moody Morgan as well: "As we thank God tonight for this great servant of the Master, we do so not to praise his powers. ... Tonight we can almost hear him say to us: 'Preach the Word; be instant in season, out of season; reprove, rebuke, exhort with all long-suffering and doctrine. ... Make full proof of thy ministry. ... I have fought the good fight, I have finished my course, I have kept the faith. ...' "

Although Howard Moody Morgan never earned an advanced theolog-ical degree (he was awarded an honorary Doctor of Divinity), he was a careful and long-standing student of the Bible, as well he must have been to have studied under his father. He also was a preacher who applied the Biblical witness to contemporary issues. A 1941 series of sermons, for example, dealt with the New Testament view of women; long before it was popular, Dr. Morgan supported the ordination of women into the ministry. Another series, preached in 1936, called for Christians to give up racial prejudice, since all persons were equal before God. A 1939 sermon attacked nationalism, or the placement of country before God. Although he loved America, he cherished the Gospel more and could be critical of his nation when he had to be, understanding that God is not necessarily an American—or even an Englishman!

The major theme in his sermons was the Incarnation, or God in Christ. His messages were always based on the Bible, for he held that it was God's Word. Yet his Biblical messages were both scholarly and often surprisingly relevant to a modern situation. He had studied Greek on his own and under G. Campbell Morgan; many times he would compose an entire sermon around a single Greek word. He had little sympathy for those who took the Scriptures out of context. He often told people that when someone once asked G. Campbell Morgan about lifting Scripture out of context, he had responded that by misreading the Bible it would be possible to justify suicide. After first quoting from one of the Gospels these words—"...and [Judas] went and hanged himself."—Dr. Morgan would conclude: "Go thou and do likewise."

The art of preaching, or proclamation of the Word, is a spoken art, one that at times seems lost today. Dr. Morgan learned this art from his father. His sermons were subtle, yet addressed to common concerns. He loved outlines: clear, concise, and direct. He used alliterations frequently to capture the ear of the listener; there was an almost poetic flow in his voice. In a very real sense, he must have understood that listening is the process by which God is apprehended. No matter the audience, there was always a sense of great urgency in his preaching, as if lives depended on the proclamation. He was somewhat disillusioned with much of contemporary preaching, feeling it either strayed from the Bible or fell into psychological lectures. He preached the power of the Risen Lord.

If his sermons had serious themes, he was far from fulfilling the image of the pious parson with long face and solemn voice. His sermons, as his life, were often full of joy—and, yes, even simple fun. There was about him the mark of a child, often amused with others but most certainly capable of laughing at himself. He seemed to have a joke for every occasion, so much so that one of his sons believed that his file cabinets were stocked with stories and jokes. He seemed to react naturally to humorous events. Once, when one of his sons let a rabbit loose in church, he remarked to the congregation: "Well, it looks as if Easter has come early this year." Another time, the joke was on him when before a Sunday School audience he asked one of his sons what Jesus rode on Palm Sunday. "Come on," he said when his son was puzzled, "it has long ears." The son's reply was swift: "Ah yes, Jesus rode into Jerusalem on a rabbit."

About 11 months before his death, he went for a visit to Massachusetts. He had grown up in Northfield, where surely he must have remembered conversations between his father and Dwight L. Moody. He went from room to room in the old Moody residence, recalling stories of his father. He stood in the pulpit where Moody had first heard the preaching of G. Campbell Morgan. It was for him a way of coming to terms with his own life and a way of saying goodbye. There was no sadness here, but rather a sense of a man who felt himself in the presence of a tradition and purpose.

The sermons collected here represent the first series of his messages to be published. Because he returned again and again to the theme of the Incarnation, it seemed logical to gather these together in one book. This was no easy task, as there were some 300 messages on Jesus alone.

The family of Dr. Morgan elected to publish some of his sermons for a number of reasons. First, it was felt that his style and message serve as a continuation of the words of G. Campbell Morgan. Second, the sermons stand on their own as testimonies to the power and meaning of Jesus for us today. Third, for students of the Bible, these messages provide an introduction to Christian thought and practice.

Today, as when Howard Moody Morgan preached, the Word takes on flesh and meaning for our lives, if we would listen.

Patricia Ruth McMillan
Richard Lyon Morgan
Mary Ann Morgan
Howard Campbell Morgan
John Crossley Morgan

I

THE CHRISTIAN LIFE AND SERVICE

The Apostle Paul offered a statement to all Christians, announcing a triumphant experience: "In all these things we are more than conquerors through Him who loved us." This is the proposal and offer of Christ to persons of every age, and this experience should distinguish the life and service of every Christian.

Every Christian sooner or later seeks to answer certain fundamental questions:

What does it mean to be a Christian?

What are the steps in entering the Christian life?

What really happens when one becomes a Christian?

What is the distinctive message of Christianity?

What is Christ's method of extending His Kingdom?

How may we best bear personal testimony?

How do we awaken the indifferent and self-satisfied?

How do we best help people whose faith is unsettled?

The first subject, then, is the gateway to the Christian life. What does it mean to be a Christian, and what are the steps in entering the Christian life?

The Scripture which can best be the basis for responding to these questions is a very revealing sentence from the lips of Christ: "And this is life eternal, that they might know thee the only true God, and Jesus Christ, whom thou hast sent." (John 17:3)

Our Lord stated it simply when He said to be a Christian is to know God and His Son Jesus Christ. To be a Christian is to be a friend of God, as He revealed Himself in the Person of Jesus.

Perhaps one of the greatest spiritual needs of our time is that of understanding what being a Christian does not mean. Many people seem to feel that believing certain dogmas means one is a Christian. It is true that one's beliefs affect one's life; hence, no one should be careless about believing. But no amount of intellectual assent to dogmas will make one a Christian. The Pharisees believed that a careful reading and memorizing of Scriptures would bring eternal life. Christ bluntly set that idea aside

1

when He said: "Search the scriptures; for in them ye think ye have eternal life: and they are they which testify of me. And ye will not come to me, that ye might have life." (John 5:39-40)

Others think that being a Christian means the experiencing of ecstatic feelings of joy and peace. No one doubts that spiritual life brings joy and peace, but waiting for such feelings has kept many persons from becoming Christians. In all our Lord's teaching He never prescribed any certain type of emotionalism as a condition of following Him.

A third group of persons hold that Christians simply follow a higher code of moral life. This seems close to what Matthew Arnold meant when he defined religion as "morality touched with emotion." While Christian life cannot be divorced from morality, it is far deeper.

A Christian is a friend of God as revealed in the person of Jesus Christ.   One must not stop with the searching of Scripture, but pass into vital fellowship with the Living Word. One must expect to have great feelings much like one might expect to experience in the presence of a friend. And because of this friendship, one must act as in the presence of a perfect friend. Christ furnishes this inner power.

If the Christian life is friendship with God through Christ, what is the gateway?

The first condition of any true friendship is that all barriers separating two persons shall be removed. Until this is done, true friendship is not possible. How is it possible to repair a broken relationship? There is one way and one way only. I must come to realize that I have done wrong and ask forgiveness. And the one wronged must grant forgiveness. We must acknowledge our wrongs before God in order that He may forgive us. "If we say that we have not sinned, we make him a liar, and his word is not in us. If we confess our sins, he is faithful and just to forgive us our sins, and to cleanse us from all unrighteousness." (I John 1:9-10)

If we are conscious of the need for forgiveness, what, then, shall we do about it? We must turn away from the wrong and decide to do right. This can be a quiet and calm act of our wills. "And when he came to himself, he said, ... Father, I have sinned against heaven, and before thee, ..." (Luke 15:17-18)

If two people wish to be friends, they must trust each other. Trust is the foundation of friendship. God has so endeavored throughout the ages to reveal Himself to us so that we will trust Him. Faith is the deliberate trust in and the active surrender of one's self to a person whose character is such as to command the soul. "And the centurion answered and said, Lord, I am not worthy that thou shouldest come under my roof; but speak the word only, and my servant shall be healed. ... When Jesus heard it, he marvelled, and said to them that followed, Verily I say unto you, I have not found so great faith, ..." (Matthew 8:8-10)

Friendship is the communion of two souls based on a harmony in the fundamental ideas of life. Friendship with Jesus means we will sit down in His presence and find what He thinks of men, of God, of sin, of joy, and of service. "Abide in me, and I in you. As the branch cannot bear fruit of itself, except it abide in the vine; no more can ye, except ye abide in me." (John 15:4)

One of the laws of friendship can be found in the expression: That which is covered and unexpressed must die. This is not a dictum of psychology but a matter of practical experience. A friendship that is not deep enough to be worth acknowledgement is a worthless matter. A serious peril of our day is that we fail to give real expression to our deepest beliefs. "And I say unto you, Whosoever shall confess me before men, him shall the Son of man also confess before the angels of God." (Luke 12:8)

If I tie my hand to my side and let it remain there for a year, it will remain lifeless. The hand has not been of service. Friendship with God in Christ means service. If I am to be your friend, I must serve you where I can. "Then Jesus answering said unto them, Go and tell John what things ye have seen and heard; how that the blind see, the lame walk, the lepers are cleansed, the deaf hear, the dead are raised, to the poor the gospel is preached." (Luke 7:22)

CHRISTIAN AFFIRMATIONS

The God of Christianity is personal. He is a conscious Being, possessed of intelligence and emotional life, which enables Him to be related with other human beings. To say God is personal does not mean He is limited. He is complete in intelligence, will, and emotional powers. He knows all truth; He is able at all times to control His actions.

The God of Christianity is self-consistent. He cannot act otherwise than in accordance with His own nature, which is in accordance with truth. There is no arbitrariness here, no whimsical capriciousness. His character is righteously self-consistent.

The God of Christianity is a Father, one who sustains toward people the loving relationship of a father. The Father desires to give each child true and full life. To this end He cares for each individual. God is no absentee creator of the universe who sits outside what happens. He is intimately connected with the daily movements of the world.

The Christian faith declares that each person is a self-conscious, free, moral being, made in God's likeness, and capable of understanding the works and manifestations of God. No other religion gives to people such high dignity. The individual is known as the friend and companion of God.

At the same time as human beings are created in the image of God, they also may elect to be in nonconformity with the will of God. Selfishness is the unwillingness to be a friend of God. And all such self-centeredness brings with it guilt—a veritable body of death.

But sin is not the last word. Christian salvation contemplates saving people from the results of sin, but it goes much deeper than freedom from punishment. Christian salvation removes the sense of guilt and the uncleanness consequent upon mankind. Grace frees the person to become right with God.

In Christ we are brought to God, our sins are forgiven, the barriers break down, and we are new creations in Him who loved us first.

THE UNIQUENESS OF THE GOSPEL

As we reconsider our Christian faith and experience, we must face the question of the uniqueness of the Christian message. What is the distinctive message of the Gospel? In order to understand clearly this uniqueness, it is necessary to state very clearly the message of non-Christian faiths.

Islam holds firmly to a personal being, who is divine and the final person in the universe. "There is no God but God" is the cry of the Islamic faith. But Islam sets forth a God who is self-existent, who acts without any regard for consistency. Of the ninety-nine names given to God of Islam, none shows the idea of fatherhood or tender care.

In Hinduism we come to an entirely different viewpoint. While Hinduism may from time to time declare God to be personal, it is a personality far different from anything we know. He is the sole essence and reality of the universe; besides this Hindu God all else is illusion— and we are mere dreams.

Buddhism tends to dismiss the concept of God as being unknowable or even unreal. In Buddhist thought there is nothing, either human or divine, which is permanent. There is no being; there is only becoming.

The beginning of Christian life may well be likened to a great awakening: the deepening of experience in the light of grace. The Bible speaks of this awakening in two great passages:

Isaiah 52:1. "Awake, awake; put on thy strength, O Zion; put on thy beautiful garments, ..."

Ephesians 5:14. "... Awake thou that sleepest, and arise from the dead, and Christ shall give thee light."

The Hebrew prophet Isaiah and the Christian Apostle Paul both use this figure of speech to call people to a new awareness of God and their service in the name of God to others.

The context of both texts is important. In Isaiah it is that portion where God is calling to His people to arouse themselves in the presence of a sinister enemy. In Chapter 51, the startling fact is that the people have cried to God saying: "Awake, awake, ... O arm of the Lord; Awake as in the ancient days, in the generations of old." (51:9) But, Isaiah reports the answer of the Lord, "Awake, awake, stand up, O Jerusalem, ..." (51:17)

In the Epistle to the Ephesians, Paul is writing to the church in Ephesus, to a church located in that strategic commercial city of that day. He is calling them out of fellowship with the works of darkness: fornication, uncleanness, covetousness, filthiness, foolish talking, and jesting. The call then comes. "Awake thou that sleepest, and arise from the dead, and Christ shall give thee light."

Two other notable events in Scripture illustrate this awakening from sleep and deadness.

Genesis 28:16. "And Jacob awaked out of his sleep, and he said, 'Surely the Lord is in this place; and I knew it not."

Luke 9:32. "... when they were awake, they saw his glory, ..."

These references to awakening are addressed to the sleep of deadness, which is to say of indifference and self-satisfaction.

The most powerful influence that can be brought to bear upon this sleep of deadness is the personality of the God-filled soul. Jesus exalted personality above all social institutions, showing that God is intensely interested in every human personality. And the real environment of human personality is that on which a person centers his ultimate attention. If one is so busy with things that he cannot cultivate fellowship with others, sooner or later he wakes up to find himself completely isolated. This type of indifference neglects to bring into the field of attention the supreme forces which make character. He who does not cultivate fellowship with God in Christ cannot possibly build true character.

A self-satisfied person commits the greatest sin against love, against the love of God who cares for all of life. In refusing to love God, this individual wounds God—and others as well.

What then is the unique cry of the Christian? Awake from sleep and death to the love of God in Christ!

II

THE GOD-MAN
OF GALILEE

THE SON OF MAN AND SIN

When we compare the work of Jesus with all He proposed to do in the world with the schemes of the earth's greatest leaders, we cannot classify Him as a mere man.

What did He think He came into the world to do? What did He consider His mission to be?

We cannot be in the least doubt of the answer, for the answer is found in His own words:

"For the Son of man is come to seek and to save that which was lost." (Luke 19:10)

"I came not to call the righteous, but sinners to repentance." (Luke 5:32)

"... I came not to judge the world, but to save the world." (John 12:47)

That Jesus should have seen evil and wanted to correct it does not necessarily set Him apart from other wise persons. The doctrine of Jesus is peculiar in that all moral evil is seen as sin, and sin is the state of being out of harmony with God's will. The evil person is at war with God; he or she loves evil more than goodness.

But Jesus came into the world to take away sin, to deliver persons from it, from its penalty and power. This is the core of His Gospel.

Jesus does not set about bettering human conditions by direct effort, through social, economic, or psychological means. He works upon the heart of human beings. Whatever improves the human condition is to be desired, but it is not enough to make mankind comfortable! Persons must be transformed. Jesus teaches that all that is truly good and needful will come to people who are delivered from sin and that no real good can come to anyone in whom sin remains. First and last, Jesus makes deliverance from sin the one needful thing—the chief good!

His doctrine is taught and illustrated in every possible way. It is in His formal discourses and His briefest comments. From His first word to the last, from the Beatitudes to The Prayer on the Cross, it is always the same thing: Man's trouble is sin; salvation only comes with deliverance from sin. The penitent Magdalene washes His feet, and He says: "... Thy sins are forgiven. ... Thy faith hath saved thee; go in peace." When Capernaum's four friends lower their neighbor into Peter's house to be healed, Jesus does not speak about the illness but rather says: "... Son, thy sins be forgiven thee."

The Incarnation separates Jesus from all other historical figures. Jesus was the Son of man for all the world, for all the human race. The evil He saw was not peculiar to one people or country, but rather part of the inner man of all nations and ages.

According to Jesus, evil and goodness are within man himself. They are not external realities but internal. For this reason, He does not dwell upon poverty or wealth, nor upon health or sickness. He is concerned about the real person, the inside and not the outside of each human being.

It is important to note as well that Jesus never speaks of a man's moral evil as mere ignorance of truth, as if instruction could remedy the situation. Sin antagonizes the heart of God, because it violates His will.

Jesus taught clearly to people that in themselves, not in their circumstances, is their real evil and their real good. Jesus came to better human beings by destroying the hold which sin has over their lives. One thing His true Disciples hate is sin. Only one thing is worth living and dying for: goodness, which is another name for Christlikeness.

THE SON OF MAN TOOK THE WAY OF PERISHING

Jesus talked of a Kingdom that was to endure forever, that was to conquer the world, and that was to bind the human race into a holy brotherhood—but He made no preparations for a successor. He told His Disciples He would die early; moreover, He indicated they would endure hardship. Other great men conceal from their followers the perils that await them. But Jesus told His friends of His suffering and sacrifice and of all that awaited them.

The text which best represents this idea is found in Luke's Gospel, Chapter 9, Verse 51: "And it came to pass, when the time was come that he should be received up, he stedfastly set his face to go to Jerusalem." This was a terrible hour in Jesus' life and work, and we should consider the time and intention of His soul.

Some have termed this time as that of Assumption, as represented in the Greek word, *analepsis*. It is important that we should clearly understand what is meant. Some suggest this word refers to His ascension, but the time had not yet come for this to happen. Jesus had come to the natural end of His life on earth. But, He steadfastly set His face to Jerusalem. Why? Because He had to go to Jerusalem and suffer many things and be killed. His cross and His giving of His life had a deep significance and power for the world. To go to the cross is not simply the way of a great man. Jesus took the way of perishing because it is God's way of establishing His Kingdom on earth. He lay down His life so that He might take it again with power. In His perishing and suffering He accomplished an act of reconciliation, atonement, and eternal significance.

NEVER MAN PLANNED LIKE THE SON OF MAN

Our text might well be the words of the officials in John 7:46: "... Never man spake ..." That was their impression as they listened. We might add, never man planned like the Son of man.

What are we to say of the means by which Jesus proposes to attain His goals—to deliver man from evil, to bring him to God, to establish a Kingdom? Yes, these, but what are His plans?

I say broadly and with some assurance that Jesus proposed none of the means often used to secure power. "Business as usual" is not His method. He utterly excluded force. His symbol is not the sword; it is the cross. Jesus does not tolerate force in carrying out His work nor persecution of any kind. Even in His hour of need He would not use force to overcome His enemies.

Neither does Jesus call upon the power of wealth to attain His end. He hardly ever spoke of money, except to warn of its dangers. He taught that greed of money is debasing. It is a man's way to bribe and buy favor. Satan believes in the power of money, so often Jesus seems "unbusinesslike."

Jesus also excludes the art of diplomacy—playing one selfishness against another. "But let your communication be, Yea, yea; Nay, nay; for whatsoever is more than these cometh of evil." (Matthew 5:37)

Jesus offers no inducement to mere self-interest. He promises absolutely nothing of the things the world loves. Neither does He base His methods upon the intellect. He does not think His Kingdom will grow by natural development or rational argument.

What, then, do His plans include?
1. Love in action.
2. Love in spirit and service.
3. Love in truth and honesty.
4. Love in purity of heart.

Humanity does not need new opinions, but new love. And this love has been shown and revealed through Jesus.

THE GALILEAN'S GRASP UPON MANKIND

Consider the influence of Jesus and it will be seen to be utterly different from all men—not in degree, but in kind. Consider the influence of Jesus from observation and consciousness.

There is the power of His teaching upon the human conscience. No words or teachings of any writer or teacher of any age that repudiate the words of Jesus have power over the conscience. The words and teachings of those who powerfully influence humanity seem to be echoes of His thought.

There is no risk of exaggeration or dogmatism here. It is right to say that Jesus holds power over the human conscience. His words and teachings illuminate the conscience.

The power of the words of Jesus is all the more powerful because of Him. There was no sin in Him. Those who believe, receive, and obey Him are changed in the spirit of life. Jesus works this miracle today—His grasp upon mankind. His true Disciples feel so much love toward Him as a person that all fear is driven out.

In summary, there are five major grasps which Jesus holds on mankind:

1. The power of His words to stir, stimulate, and enlighten the conscience.

2. His own great character incarnating, expounding His doctrine.

3. The absolute universality of His character.

4. The change of heart Jesus brings to pass.

5. The love of His Disciples for Him until this very hour.

III

THE ANSWERS OF CHRIST
TO THE QUESTIONS OF MEN

The four Gospels record approximately ninety questions being asked of Jesus. What is of supreme importance, moreover, is that we have a record of these answers of Christ to the questions of men.

All the questions addressed to Jesus were not of equal value, but the great majority were significant inquiries after His Truth—and they received all-important answers from our Lord. It is only necessary to recall the many times in the four Gospels the little, but vital, phrase occurs, "And Jesus answered, ..."

Moreover, the student of the Bible is immediately impressed with the fact that again and again the questions asked of Jesus then are still the questions of persons today.

There are some general conclusions which can be drawn by reviewing the answers of Jesus to the questions of men. First, Jesus generally answered any question, even when it was prompted by evil. Second, Jesus frequently responded to a question by asking another question, thus making persons reflect upon themselves. Third, Jesus is reported as once making no response at all. This was in the case of Herod, when Jesus "... answered him nothing." Fourth, Jesus produced a profound impression with His answers.

For sake of clarity, the answers of Jesus can be grouped into five general categories:
1. The answers to the questions of His Disciples.
2. The answers to the questions of rulers.
3. The answers to questions of the underworld of evil.
4. The answers to certain individuals.
5. The answers to the multitudes.

THE ANSWERS OF JESUS ABOUT SALVATION

There are two major questions of salvation asked by the Disciples of Jesus:

Luke 13:22-30. The question was asked: "Lord, are there few that be saved?" The answer of Jesus reveals to us His teaching, and the first part of the answer begins in a striking manner: "... many, I say unto you, will seek to enter in, and shall not be able."

Matthew 19:23-30. Our Lord was making a comment about the rich, young ruler when he said: "... Verily I say unto you, That a rich man shall hardly enter into the kingdom of heaven." His Disciples had asked the question: Who then can be saved? His answer was direct: "With men this is impossible; but with God all things are possible."

Jesus rarely used the word salvation, but this concept is everywhere in His teaching. More than once He said that the Son of man had come to save that which was lost. This thought not only postulates a condition of loss and peril, but also proclaims a way of redemption.

There were two occasions during His ministry when His Disciples raised questions about salvation.

In Luke's account, we see that Jesus had been on His way through cities and villages when someone asked: Are there few that can be saved? It was a sincere, but speculative question, prompted by the fact that many were refusing Him. It may also have been a question from someone who was anxious about his own salvation. But, it is still a question of many Christians.

Jesus gave an emphatic answer to the question: "Strive to enter in at the strait gate: ..." In reality he responded: Don't waste your time debating that question; look to yourself. His answer was then: First be sure of your own salvation, and there will be many who come in the Kingdom.

In Matthew's account, the Disciples asked: Who then can be saved? They asked this after Jesus had said it was hard for a rich man to enter the Kingdom.

As we recall His words in the Sermon on the Mount, we can understand why it is hard for a rich man to enter the Kingdom: "Blessed are the poor in spirit: ..." Wealth means power, and power creates pride.

Who then can be saved? Let us not do an injustice to the Disciples by the way we interpret that question. The popular interpretation holds that if a rich man cannot be saved, then who can? The answer of Jesus is clear. "... With men it is impossible, but not with God: ..."

And, at the close of this answer of Christ, we have another question of Peter: "... Lo, we have left all, what then shall we have?" It was a daring question, still in the realm of salvation. We need not be angry at Peter for such a question. We do well to notice that Jesus was not angry but gave a word of warning. "... Verily I say unto you, That ye which have followed me, in the regeneration when the Son of man shall sit in the throne of his glory, ye also shall sit upon twelve thrones, judging the twelve tribes of Israel."

There is an abiding answer made by Jesus to the question of salvation: Salvation is through God alone, through His Son, and is a free gift to those who enter the narrow door.

QUESTIONS ABOUT HIS PARABLES

There are three occasions in the Gospels when Jesus provided answers to questions of His Disciples about His parables.

Matthew 13:0, Mark 4:10, Luke 8:9. All three Evangelists report that on the day our Lord uttered the Parable of the Sower His Disciples asked Him a question. Matthew reports the question as: "... Why speakest thou unto them in parables?"

Matthew 13:36. The second question came on the same day as the first. "... Declare unto us the parable of the tares of the field."

Luke 12:41. The third question about His parables was asked by Peter: "Lord, speakest thou this parable unto us, or even to all?"

The answers of Jesus to His Disciples about the parables can be considered under two points: (1) the answers to the question about the reason for His parabolic method and (2) the answers which He gave to certain parables.

Why did Jesus speak in parables? Let us recall the time and circumstance when the question was asked. It is evident that at this point in His public ministry Jesus began to use this method; from this point on, He developed the parabolic method.

The first part of His answer is found in the words, "... Because it is given unto you to know the mysteries of the kingdom of heaven, but to them it is not given." The difference lay in the fact that His Disciples had received Christ as Master, while others had rejected Him. "Therefore I speak to them in parables." Here is the infinite pity of God revealed in Jesus: A great teacher arrests His hearers with a story.

But what is a parable? A parable means something placed by the side of something else in order to explain one thing by another. The parables were pictures of realities seen and known, but intended to reveal and explain realities unseen and often unknown. Jesus did not use parables to conceal truth, but rather to capture the imagination and proclaim the Good News of God's Kingdom.

The further answer of Jesus to why He used parables was also His explanation of the Parable of the Sower. His teaching revealed the four different soils, or the reasons why people either rejected or received the Good News. There is the wayside where persons have not depth and do not receive the Word. There are rocky places where people are quick to receive the Word but then cannot endure the tribulations that follow. There is thorny ground where individuals hear the Word but are choked by the cares and riches of this world. And there is the good ground where the seeds yield fruit.

In the Parable of the Tares, Jesus provides another answer. This parable was about the sowing of the Evil One while men slept. The owner of the field commands his servants not to root up the tares but wait until they grow so that they can be gathered and burned.

In this parable Jesus instructs His Disciples that the method of evil in this world is to imitate the Kingdom. As the good seed is sown, the evil seed is also sown. But, at the time of the harvest, the evil will finally be destroyed.

There are three major conclusions that can be drawn from His answers to questions about the parables:

1. His use of parables is an indication that the People of God must use every right and good means to waken others to the Good News of His Kingdom.

2. His explanation of the Parable of the Sower is that we shall always encounter difficulties in our work for Him.

3. His explanation of the Parable of the Tares is that, while we recognize the presence of evil, we also know that there is to be a day of harvest when evil shall finally be destroyed.

ANSWERS TO QUESTIONS ABOUT GREATNESS AND FORGIVENESS

There are two answers to two questions about greatness and forgiveness, as recorded in the Eighteenth Chapter of Matthew. The questions and answers are found together as they occurred on the same occasion in the midst of His teaching to His Disciples.

The question was asked of Him, "Who is the greatest in the kingdom of heaven?"

The Disciples were listening to His teaching about His new Kingdom. But they had noticed a contrast between their idea of the Kingdom and His idea of the Kingdom. They had looked for a Kingdom upon the pattern of the material—with the gradations of office of king, officers, and on down.

Jesus answered somewhat differently than they expected. He called to them a little child and set him in the midst of them. A startling and dramatic answer by way of action!

First of all is the action. "... Jesus called a little child unto him, and set him in the midst of them." The answer to their question: Everyone is great within the Kingdom. There are no little souls, setting aside thoughts of class, riches, and race. The spirit of the child is trust, humility, and sincere beliefs. All of these are of greatness.

But what is said about forgiveness? Peter thought he had suggested the greatest heights when he said a person should be forgiven seven times. But the answer was: "Jesus said unto him ... seventy times seven." And He concluded that God would not forgive us until we forgive our brothers and sisters from our hearts.

QUESTIONS ABOUT THE FIRE AND SWORD

There are two questions of the Disciples about fire and the sword. The first question was asked by James and John, the sons of thunder: "... Lord, wilt thou that we command fire to come down from heaven, and consume them, ..." But Jesus turned and rebuked them. The second question was asked by the Disciples in the Garden of Gethsemane: "... Lord, shall we smite [them] with the sword?" And Jesus responded, "Suffer ye [them] thus far."

It is important to study these two questions and answers in greater detail.

The first answer is recorded in Luke 9:51-56. Certain Disciples had been sent into a Samaritan village to make ready for Him. Christ was going to Jerusalem. In response to the Disciples' question about whether fire should be sent, Jesus responded: "... the Son of man is not come to destroy men's lives, but to save them." In the spirit of His cross, He could not countenance the spirit of fire. There was no place for revenge.

The second answer of Jesus takes place in the Garden of Gethsemane where Judas betrays Him with a kiss, and one of His Disciples asked: "Lord, shall we smite [them] with a sword?" The calm words of Jesus follow: "Suffer ye [them] thus far." And then He healed the man who had been injured, the last act of divine surgery performed by the compassionate hands of Jesus made necessary by the blundering zeal of one of His Disciples.

The heart of His response is in His hope that the Scriptures might be fulfilled. He had come to His hour—to die for the sake of the world—and not by violence done to others. Had not He said earlier in the same garden: "... But now, he that hath a purse, let him take *it*, likewise *his* scrip: and he that hath no sword, let him sell his garment, and buy one."

The Kingdom of God cannot come with harshness, tyranny, or violence. We cannot say to those who reject Jesus: Let us force Him upon you! We cannot point to those who do not believe and are full of pride and call them wrong and inferior! The second great answer of Jesus was that the heart of His mission was love, that this involved the cross, and that there was no use fighting against God's plan.

Jesus rejected the sword and fire. He hated violence. He sought out the path of redeeming love.

THE QUESTION OF CASTING OUT EVIL

At the foot of the mountain, in the valley, a company of people are waiting the coming of Jesus and three of His Disciples. Jesus has taken

Peter, James, and John to the mountain where He has been transfigured before them. This is one of the great hours in His life. He has come to the end of His perfect existence, and His glory shines as a great light.

In the valley below, nine Disciples are face to face with a tragic situation. A demon-possessed boy, the only son of his bewildered father, is before them. And there also are critics of the Disciples.

Our Lord utters a solitary cry: "O faithless and perverse generation, how long shall I be with you? ..." Jesus talks with God and then commands the evil spirit to come out of the boy.

The Disciples, who could not cast out the evil, then ask a natural question: Why could we not cast out this evil? And Jesus responds simply: "Because of your unbelief: for verily I say unto you, If ye have faith as a grain of mustard seed, ye shall say unto this mountain, Remove hence to yonder place; and it shall remove; ..."

By faith, did Jesus mean simply an intellectual assent to Him? By prayer did He mean these men should have taken time to recite memorized phrases? No, by faith He meant a commitment to God; by prayer he meant a sustained fellowship with God.

All too often today the picture of the church is one of helplessness before evil. Are we honest enough to come before Jesus to ask Him why we are afraid?

The answer of Jesus to our question is straightforward. Lack of faith in Jesus is the paralysis that blocks our response to the needs of the world. And the lack of a sustained relationship with God is our loss of power to combat evil.

When we hear God and obey Him, we will walk with Him in power. But His way is the way of suffering, the way of the cross, and the way of sacrifice.

THE RESPONSE OF JESUS ABOUT BREAD FOR THE HUNGRY

The answers of our Lord to the questions of His Disciples about bread for the hungry are found in Mark 6:30-34 and Mark 8:1-9.

After the Disciples had returned from their mission of visiting surrounding towns and cities, Jesus called them to a desert place to rest awhile. The great crowds followed Him on foot. This occasion is recorded by all four Evangelists. In John's account, we read of the boy with his lunch and that Jesus used the miracle as an outward sign of the great teaching, *I am the bread of life.*

When the Disciples wanted to send people away to eat, Jesus asked simply, "... How many loaves have ye? ..." He then took what they had and fed the multitude.

His Disciples' questions reveal two continuing sins of the heart: lack of compassion for the hungry and lack of faith in the power of God to respond to human needs.

What does the response of Jesus mean?

1. Jesus cares for the physical hunger of people.

2. Jesus expects His Disciples to share what they have with others.

3. Jesus expects us to share what we have, no matter how small, with others.

4. Jesus believes that what physical bread is to the body, the Gospel is to the life of the spirit.

5. Jesus commands us to give what we have to Him and to others in His name.

QUESTIONS ABOUT HIS FATHER

The answers of our Lord to the questions of a company of Jews who asked him a number of questions about His Father reveals His teaching about God.

The entire discussion of Jesus with these people is recorded in the Gospel of John, Chapter 8, Verses 12-39. The atmosphere is one of opposition, questioning, and discussion. It is a striking illustration of His patience as He answers different questions.

The discussion begins with a great claim by Jesus. "... I am the light of the world. ..." He proclaims. This is followed by two sublime statements: "... he that followeth me shall not walk in darkness, ..." and "... [he] shall have the light of life. ..."

The first discussion began with the charge of the people, "... Thou bearest record of thyself; ..." They were quoting Him, "If I bear witness of myself, my witness is not true." (John 5:31) Jesus replied that His witness was based on certain knowledge. He and the Father were united. He was not speaking alone.

The second discussion began with a bitter comment: "Where is thy father?" Mocking Him, they said: Produce your father; where is he?

The third discussion centered around a word of condemnation: "... I go my way, and ye shall seek me, and shall die in your sins: ..." The Jews then were angry. "... Who art thou?" they asked. And Jesus replied, "... I do always those things that please Him."

There are seven questions asked of Jesus during this discussion:

1. Where is the Father?

2. Who are you?

3. How can you say that you shall be made free?

4. Say we not that we well know Thou art a Samaritan and hast a devil?

5. Are you greater than Abraham?

6. Who made thee?
7. Have you seen Abraham?

All of these questions came from the people, and all of them pointed toward the relationship of Jesus to God. Some of the questions are sincere; others are angry and bitter. What does Jesus respond?

1. The Father and Son are one.
2. His response is from the Father.
3. Through His power, all people will be made free.
4. Through His works and words, God is affirmed.
5. He is the Word of God made incarnate.

THE ANSWERS ABOUT JOHN THE BAPTIST

John the Baptist was born of devout parents, both of them from priestly ancestry. It was written of them that "... they were both righteous before God, walking in all the commandments and ordinances of the Lord ..." John's birth is reported to have taken place under remarkable circumstances. John was probably older than Jesus and went into the wilderness in preparation for his ministry. "And the child grew, and waxed strong in spirit, and was in the deserts till the day of his shewing unto Israel."

John's public ministry began as one crying in the wilderness; his essential message was one of repentance before God. His fiery message to the people was: "... the axe is laid unto the root of the trees. ... but one mightier than I cometh, ... he shall baptize you with the Holy Ghost and with Fire: Whose fan is in his hand, and he will throughly purge his floor, and will gather the wheat into his garner; but the chaff he will burn with fire unquenchable."

Such was the man and such was his message.

The first question of John came during the dramatic days of his ministry in the wilderness. Great crowds were coming to hear him. And it was written: "Then cometh Jesus from Galilee to Jordan unto John, to be baptized of him."

When John saw Jesus and realized He had come also to be baptized, instantly he knew who He was and hesitated with a question "... Comest thou to me?" From John's vantage point there was no place for repentance and baptism for Jesus. But Jesus wanted to be identified with the sinful, perhaps to fulfill the prophecy of Isaiah, "... he was numbered with the transgressors; ..."

In the response of Jesus to John there is another prophecy. And this prophecy was of His passion as the great redeeming act of His mission.

The second question to Jesus came from John when he was in prison. "... Art thou he that should come? or look we for another?" It was an honest question of perplexity from the heart of faith. There is profound insight in the last phrase, "... look we for another?" If Jesus was not the Messiah, John still believed that God's will would be fulfilled.

The response of Jesus to John's question is a beacon for us today as well. "Go your way, and tell John what things ye have heard and seen; how that the blind see, the lame walk, the lepers are cleansed, the deaf hear, the dead are raised, to the poor the gospel is preached." In the last sentence Jesus linked the account of His work with a great prophetic word which John would understand: "... to the poor the gospel is preached." This word from Isaiah was the same portion Jesus had cited in the synagogue in Nazareth at the inauguration of His ministry.

The message of Jesus to John is one concerning the method of His ministry of grace until the Day of Judgment comes. "... art thou he that should come? ..." Yes, is the response of Jesus.

THE ANSWER OF JESUS TO THE QUESTION OF GOD'S CARE

Sometimes Jesus did not answer a question with words, but rather with deeds. Such is the case at an occasion reported by John at the sickness and death of Lazarus. In the home at Bethany, Jesus was always an honored and loved guest. It is written that Jesus "... loved Martha, and her sister [Mary], and Lazarus." To the home of these three devoted friends, Jesus came for quietness and strength. During his last week, each night He retired from Jerusalem to Bethany.

Lazarus had fallen sick, and the sisters had sent for Jesus. He had not come in time. Lazarus had died. When Jesus finally arrived and went with Mary and Martha to the place where Lazarus was buried, we find one of the most poignant phrases in the Bible: "Jesus wept." And some of the people said, "... Behold, how he loved him!" And it was at this moment that a question was asked, perhaps not directly of Jesus, but loud enough for Him to hear. "... Could not this man, which opened the eyes of the blind, have caused that even this man should not have died?"

Here is the persistent problem, which can be stated in the form of another question: Does God care? Could Jesus, in other words, have prevented the death of Lazarus?

Jesus did not respond with words. But the whole story is His answer to this kind of question. It is important to remember that when the news of Lazarus' death reached Jesus, He had said to His Disciples: "... I am glad for your sakes that I was not there, to the intent ye may believe; ..." The whole answer is found in the words: "... for your sakes; ..." In order to understand this, we must see it on two planes of consciousness. First, this sickness of Lazarus is not unto death, for whosoever believes in me shall never die. And second, Lazarus is dead. Take away the stone, lose him, and let him go. Here are the two planes: the eternal truth of the everlasting soul and the physical death of the body.

Could Jesus have prevented the death of Lazarus? The answer is yes. Could he have prevented this death in the realm of motive and purpose. No, no he could not! There was something greater than having the illness cured: the restoration from death.

Does God care? The answer is yes. He is doing something. In the midst of your suffering and despair, He is giving new life. In the midst even of death we abide with God, even as He abides with us.

THE QUESTION OF THE RICH, YOUNG RULER

It is important to note that the question of the rich, young ruler had been asked before and received a different answer. In Luke 10:25 we read: "And, behold, a certain lawyer stood up, and tempted him, saying, Master, what shall I do to inherit eternal life?" The question was one that tested Jesus. But in Mark 10:17-22 we have the same question asked with a different motive: "And when he was gone forth into the way, there came one running, and kneeled to him, and asked him, Good Master, what shall I do that I may inherit eternal life?"

The rich, young ruler was not primarily asking about how to get to heaven. The words—eternal life—may be translated as "age abiding life." The question was addressed to the quality of life, both here and hereafter.

The answer to this question moves along three lines, each of them part of His answer and all leading to His full answer.

First, Jesus said: "... Why callest thou me good? there is none good but one, that is, God." Abruptly, Jesus challenged the mind, saying: Why do you kneel to Me, when it is God who is Lord? Second, Jesus responded: "Thou knowest the commandments, ..." Here is an emotional appeal to the young ruler. If the man knows the commandments of God, why does he need to ask the question? And third, Jesus responds: "... go thy way, sell whatsoever thou hast, and give to the poor, and thou shalt have treasure in heaven: and come, take up the cross, and follow me." The answer here is to follow Him. We know the rich, young ruler, burdened by his possessions, could not follow. Today, others take the same path. But, it is a path that is not of God's choosing. To follow Jesus one must give everything for the sake of His Gospel.

WHY IS THERE SUFFERING?

During the time when Jesus was present in Jerusalem at the feast of the tabernacles, there is a story about a man who was blind from birth. Jesus saw the man, possibly sitting as a beggar asking alms. And the Disciples asked Jesus: Who sinned, this man or his parents? If he is blind, he must have sinned, or his parents must have.

The Disciples surely felt there was a connection between physical disability and sin, as was the common thought of that time. No person was ever born blind without having committed some sin.

But Jesus answered: "... Neither hath this man sinned, nor his parents: but that the works of God should be made manifest in him." Jesus did not give any answer, except to dismiss the Disciples' responses.

But He did add more, "... that the works of God should be made manifest in him." Jesus did not mean that this man had to be born blind in order for God to work. But He does declare His mission of removing the disability.

When we are faced with innocent suffering, what is our answer? We must sometimes face the fact that at times there appears to be no answer if one considers it intellectually. But we are told to remove the cause of the suffering, as best we can, and bring relief to those who suffer. If we cannot supply a final answer to the cause of suffering, we can at least ease the suffering. And if we do not make the attempt, we do not walk with Jesus.

THE ANSWERS OF JESUS ABOUT THE SABBATH

Jesus was in continual conflict with the religious rulers over the question of the Sabbath. In fact, it was over questions of this kind that the rulers decided that Jesus should be killed.

It is important to recall something about these rulers who opposed Him. The order of the scribes had their origin in the time of Ezra; and then, a little later on, in the time of the Maccabees, the order of the Pharisees sprang up. These rulers were to interpret the laws of God, but they also added their own traditions. There were, for example, thirty-nine prohibitions to interpret the one law *Thou Shalt Do No Work*. These traditions became part of the law.

There are two occasions when Jesus spoke about the Sabbath. On the first occasion, the Pharisees said: "Why do ye that which is not lawful to do on the sabbath days?" Mark tells us that the question was addressed to Jesus Himself. On the second occasion, the question was more sinister: "Is it lawful to do good on the sabbath days? ..." This question was asked to trap Jesus.

In response to these questions, Jesus assumed full responsibility for the action of His Disciples. He reminded the questioners of what David did, by eating on the Sabbath. He also reminded them that God desired mercy, not sacrifice, freeing the Sabbath for God and not mankind.

WHAT IS THE AUTHORITY OF JESUS?

All three of the Evangelists record Jesus responding to questions about his authority. It was a question asked by many including official delega-

The Maxwell Street Presbyterian Church on the campus of the University of Kentucky where Dr. Morgan served from 1927 through 1932.

Succeeding his father, G. Campbell Morgan, in 1932, Howard Moody Morgan preached at the Tabernacle Presbyterian Church, Philadelphia, for 18 years.

Howard Moody Morgan, 1925, during his years in Lexington, Kentucky.

Three generations, 1930, (left to right): Howard Moody Morgan, G. Campbell Morgan, and Richard Morgan.

Howard Moody Morgan, 1955.

Westminster Chapel, England, is the site of the annual Campbell Morgan Memorial Lecture series. Howard Moody Morgan delivered a lecture here during the series in 1963.

tions of the rulers, chief priests, scribes, and representatives of the Sanhedrin. When the question was first asked, it was full of malice and a desire to trap him. In the centuries following, however, it has become a central theological question: By what authority did Jesus claim to be the Son of God?

On Monday of Holy Week, Jesus had entered the temple and cleansed it of those who profaned the name of God. This action precipitated the coming together of rulers to question Jesus about His authority. This was an official act, since previously they had listened to Him, always on the fringe of a crowd. The dark forces which opposed Jesus were fourfold: unbelief that questioned His authority, worldliness which questioned whether taxes should be paid, rationalism which questioned future life, and intellectual dishonesty that questioned the Great Commandment.

Who gave you this authority? This was the question. Is it political, social, or spiritual?

Jesus responded to their question by asking them one in return. He told them He was willing to answer their question if they answered His. "The baptism of John, was it from heaven, or of men?" They were now faced with a decision. And Jesus knew that if they had been blind to the evidences of John's mission, they would be more blind to His. And Jesus then asked another question with a parable. The parable was the story of the two sons of a father. The one son said he would obey, yet he disobeyed; the other said he would disobey, but he repented and did the will of his father.

In reality, Jesus referred the questioners back to John. What had John said about the authority of Jesus? "... Behold the Lamb of God, which taketh away the sin of the world." Jesus, in other words, spoke and acted in accordance with God's will. The authority of the God-man is from His father.

THE QUESTIONS ABOUT ALLEGIANCE TO THE STATE

There are two important scenes in which Jesus teaches about the relationship of allegiance to state and fidelity to God. Both of these scenes are recorded in the Gospel of Matthew (17:24-27 and 22:15-22).

The first occasion, or scene, was recorded only by Matthew, and the place was Capernaum. "Doth not your teacher pay tribute?" It was a question of some of the rulers. It was addressed indirectly to Jesus, but directly to His Disciples. This tax was not a Roman one, but a Temple tax. Some of the Disciples had paid this tax, but not Jesus. The answer of Jesus to this question moves along three lines: a claim, a concession, and a command.

Jesus asked Peter about the paying of tribute. Do the kings of the earth receive taxes from their children or from strangers? When Peter replied strangers, Jesus said: "Then are the children free." His claim here was that

He was the Son of God and thereby free of Temple taxes. But His concession to Peter was that he should go to the sea and catch a fish, so that the rulers would not have cause to stumble. And finally, His command to Peter was: "... take, and give unto them for me and thee."

On yet another occasion, Jesus dealt with the question of paying taxes in which He indicates His attitude toward the state. This scene is recorded by all three Evangelists.

A coalition of religious groups approached Jesus, asking him: "Is it lawful to give tribute unto Caesar, or not?" It was a clever question, calculated to place Jesus in a double bind between the religious and political authorities. If He said yes, it would fan the fires of those who hated the Roman rule. And if he said no, then His enemies could report Him to the Roman government as a traitor.

Jesus responded in a penetrating fashion by first asking a question in return: "Why tempt ye me, ye hypocrites?" He knew the insincerity of the questioners. Then, with calmness, He asked for a coin. On one side of the coin was the face of Caesar Tiberius and on the other side were two words, Pontifex Maximus (the greatest potentate). His answer was direct: "Render therefore unto Caesar the things which are Caesar's; and unto God the things that are God's."

The first part of His answer was that they were using Caesar's coinage, thus accepting his protection. They should be honest enough to admit this and pay for it. The second part of His answer reminded the leaders of a higher law. While paying taxes, they should remember their supreme allegiance to God. Jesus passed beyond all political realities and declared that worldly authority was secondary to God's laws. More than once in history, persons have broken their allegiance to the state because of a higher authority. When someone says, therefore, that they love their country above all else, they are disobeying the commandment of Jesus. The true basis of citizenship is devotion to God, whose Kingdom is not political.

ANSWERS ABOUT THE GREATEST COMMANDMENT

It was Tuesday of His last week before the cross—the day of controversy with the rulers in Jerusalem. The Pharisees asked the question: "Master, what is the great commandment in the law?"

This was a burning question of many. Some said a rigid observance of the Sabbath was the heart of the law. Schools and parties formed to interpret the law. Religious leaders debated obscure and often unimportant rituals, as we do today.

Earlier, it should be remembered that there had been a question: "... what shall I do to inherit eternal life?" To which Jesus had responded,

"... What is written in the law? how readest thou?" To which the questioner replied: "Thou shalt love ... God ... and thy neighbour ..."

Jesus exposed the heart of faith in His response. Everything is reduced to a basic principle: love of God and humanity. Love God: This immediately dispenses with intellectual gymnastics and theological nit-picking. But love of God is often misunderstood. I am thinking of the great masses of persons outside and inside the church who reverently worship God but do not love Him. They think of God as a king, jealous, and capricious in His dealings with mankind and coldly immoral and uninvolved. But Jesus said: God is love. The whole Bible harmonizes with that truth. The New Testament makes love everywhere the source of God's power and our hope. Without love of God, the law of religion is a shame and a chain around our necks.

The second commandment of Jesus is linked to the first, and together the two form the heart of religious faith. We are to love our neighbor as ourselves. How do I love myself? My love of self becomes all it ought to be when I passionately desire to be all God intended me to be. The love of neighbor is not sentimental attachment nor a weakening of power. It is the power of God dwelling in me when I love my neighbor, who is the person in need.

Rightly understood, Jesus has responded to the question about the greatest commandment. We might also say he replied to the nagging question: In what does true religion consist?

In our day, the answers to the question of true religion are as contradictory as they were in the time of Jesus. "True religion consists in belonging to the true church," we are told by an amazing number of people. And it follows, upon closer examination, that they mean their church to be the only true one. Beyond this church, all others are in error. Another group holds that true religion is bound up with a true partaking of the sacraments. The proper person must, in the proper way, administer the proper sacrament. Without this, there can be no communion with God. There are still others who believe that true religion is assent to correct doctrine—and, of course, they hold claim to the only correct version. God forbid that we should make so little of the church and its sacraments that they become ends rather than means to faith, an end creating division within the Body of Christ.

Jesus casts aside our petty quarrels by reaching for the heart of God and humanity. Love God. Leave the petty controversies outside His House. Love your neighbors, for whom Jesus died.

THE ANSWERS OF JESUS TO NICODEMUS

The Biblical record of the conversations of Jesus with Nicodemus is contained in the Third Chapter of the Gospel According to John. As far as we know, this represents the only time the two met. Two other occasions in the New Testament report the presence of Nicodemus. One is when, in meeting with the Sanhedrin, he spoke in defense of Jesus. A second reference is found after the cross: "And there came also Nicodemus, which at the first came to Jesus by night, ..." (John 19:39)

In John 3, however, we face a momentous meeting with Nicodemus when he asked three questions. It is important to note the character of this man who came to Jesus at night and talked with him. He was a Pharisee, a ruler, and an honest man. He asked three questions of Jesus: How can a man be born again? Can he enter a second time into his mother's womb? How can these things be?

The question is thus: How can a person go back to the beginning and live in the power of a new life? I am the result of all that I was yesterday, the day before, and all the yesterdays since my birth.

The first answer of Jesus to Nicodemus said in effect, "... Except a man be born of water and of the Spirit, ..." This is a reference to John's baptism. The symbol of water implies repentance and regeneration. The first birth is of the flesh; the second birth is of the spirit. New birth, therefore, while impossible in a physical sense, is possible in a spiritual sense. Jesus illustrated this by citing the blowing of the wind. We know the power of the wind and act upon it, even if it is mysterious and without physical visibility.

In the answers of Jesus there is a declaration of two essential Christian principles. First, it is only from the illumination of a new birth that there can be escape from darkness. Second, the possibility of new birth is made possible by God.

THE QUESTIONS OF PILATE

Pilate is mentioned by all four Evangelists in the trial of Jesus; he is also mentioned as being governor when John began his ministry and one other time in connection with the murder of certain Galileans. Pilate is spoken of three times in the Book of Acts and once in Paul's letter to Timothy. Pilate owes his principal fame to his contact with Jesus.

For obvious reasons, Pilate is not seen in a positive light by the writers of the New Testament. He is seen as a man of haughty disposition, a contemptuous man, but with some pity and with an inquiring mind.

The questions of Pilate to Jesus take place inside and outside of his palace. There are eight questions recorded.

1. Art thou the King of the Jews? Jesus responded by asking Pilate if this was his own personal inquiry or had others prompted him to ask it.

2. Am I a Jew?

3. What hast thou done? Jesus responded by telling Pilate that His Kingdom was not of this world.

4. Art thou a king then? Jesus replied by telling Pilate that He came as a witness to truth.

5. What is truth? Jesus did not respond.

6. Whence art thou? Jesus did not respond.

7. Speakest thou not unto me?

8. Knowest thou not that I have power to release thee and have power to crucify thee? Jesus responded: "Thou couldest have no power at all against me, except it were given thee from above: ..."

The questions of Pilate are revealing for they are thoughts that face every person from time to time. The answers of Jesus reveal the essence of who He was. My Kingdom is not of this world. To this end I was born and to this end am I come into the world that I should bear witness to the truth. I am the truth, the way, and the life.

THE ANSWERS OF JESUS TO HEROD

In three brief sentences the dealing of Jesus with Herod can be summarized. He avoided him. He sent him a message of stinging satire. He refused to speak with him.

There is much known about Herod, both from Biblical and other sources. He was the son of Herod, commonly called the Great, and of Malthace, who was a Samaritan woman. Thus, Herod was part Samaritan. He came to be known as the king of the Jews. It was a title he personally coveted, granted to him by Rome. He was often described as "utterly evil" by his contemporaries. He was also a sensual man, in the worst sort of way. At the time of Jesus, he was living with his brother's wife, who was also his niece.

There are three major references to Herod in the New Testament.

The first reference to Herod concerns the murder of John the Baptist. In the account in Matthew, the writer ends by citing the attitude of Herod when he heard about Jesus. "... This is John the Baptist; he is risen from the dead ..." Herod was among the number who went to hear John. All Judea was going out to hear John, and probably Herod was among that group. This contact may have convinced Herod that John was a holy man. Moreover, as Mark reports, Herod "... heard him gladly." It is this same conclusion Mark reached when he wrote "... the common people heard him gladly." It was during this time that Herod openly took his brother's wife. John the Baptist denounced this act, and the woman, Herodias, hated John for this reason. When he imprisoned John, Herod intended to save him from this woman's wrath. But Herod went back on his intention. Inflamed by alcohol, he told the daughter of Herodias that he would give her anything she wanted. She, in consultation with her mother, wanted the head of John the Baptist.

A second reference to Herod is found in Luke, when the Pharisees came to Jesus telling him that Herod wanted to kill him. There can be little doubt that their report was accurate. Their advice to Jesus was that he should flee. But Jesus sent Herod a biting message of scorn: "... Go ye, and tell that fox, Behold, I cast out devils, and I do cures to day and to morrow, and the third day I shall be perfected." Jesus had no intention of bowing to evil.

The third reference to Herod is found in Luke, at a time when Jesus met him. It was the day of His trial. Pilate sent Jesus to Herod, who hoped Jesus would perform some miracle for him. But Jesus said nothing to Herod. Shortly thereafter, Herod had his soldiers mock Jesus.

What does it mean that Jesus said nothing to Herod? Herod was morally and spiritually dead. Nothing Jesus could do or say would have any impact. By His silence, Jesus spoke loudly about Herod, reserving for him the retribution of God. In the face of evil, the Son of man refuses to play by the rules. The silence of Jesus is not a passive act but rather an active condemnation of the powers of this world.

QUESTIONS TO THE RISEN LORD

After His resurrection Jesus appeared only to those who loved Him. If He was crucified in public, He returned privately to His followers. There are four recorded answers of the Risen Lord:

1. His answer to the questions of the two Disciples on the Emmaus Road.
2. His answer to the question of Peter about John.
3. His answers to the questions about the coming Kingdom.
4. His answer to the question of Saul, who later became Paul.

Luke, with accustomed beauty, writes of the resurrection, giving certain events of the day. It is an account of the light that changed the darkness into glory.

The events chosen took place in the early morning, the afternoon, and the evening. The place was the dusty road leading from Jerusalem to Emmaus, a distance of about seven miles. The people were two Disciples; one is named Cleopas and the other is unnamed. There is a suggestion by some scholars that it might have been Luke himself, but we do not know this from the record. The third person in this encounter was the Risen Lord.

The two Disciples had been walking along the road, talking with each other. Jesus came among them, asking: What are the two of you discussing? His question amazed them. "... Art thou only a stranger in Jerusalem, and hast not known the things which are come to pass there in these days?" one of them responds. When Jesus asked them to elaborate, they poured out their hearts to Him, saying they had hoped this Jesus would be the person who would redeem Israel. Jesus responded with a gentle rebuke: "O fools, and slow of heart to believe all that the prophets have spoken: ..." He continued with a question, "... Ought not Christ to have suffered these things, and to enter in his glory?" He concluded by interpreting for them all that had been said about Him from the prophets.

When they arrived in Emmaus, they asked Him to stay with them. While they were eating dinner, He took the bread and blessed it, broke it, and gave it to them. Then he vanished from their sight, as they remarked to one another: "... Did not our heart burn within us by the way, and while he opened to us the scriptures?" Then they walked back to Jerusalem to announce the glad tidings: "... The Lord is risen indeed, ..."

There is an abiding message in the Risen Lord's answer. He walks beside us all the way of our journey, even unto death. And when the journey ends we shall see Him face to face, and this vision shall grow more glorious than the brightest light.

THE RISEN LORD AMONG HIS DISCIPLES

John 21 begins with the words, "After these things Jesus shewed himself again ..." John clearly indicates this to be an appearance of Jesus to His Disciples.

Seven Disciples were together; they had spent the night fishing and had caught nothing. In the morning, a stranger hailed them from the beach and gave them instructions where to cast their nets. There followed a huge haul of fish, and they recognized Jesus.

Around the breakfast prepared by Jesus they found warmth and comfort. Then Jesus asked Peter: "... lovest thou me ..." And Peter answered, "... thou knowest that I love thee." Our Lord used the word agapao, meaning a steadfast devotion. Peter used another word, phileo, which meant affectionate regard. The third time Jesus used the second word, and Peter was grieved. Jesus then gave Peter a commission: "... Feed my sheep." The Risen Lord then ended the conversation with His familiar words: "... Follow me." The words are full of meaning. Travel with me; come by my side. Join in the way. It was at this moment that Peter asked Jesus a question, seeing another Disciple whom Jesus had loved: "... Lord, and what shall this man do?"

Jesus responded to Peter quickly. "... If I will that he tarry till I come, what is that to thee? follow thou me." In other words, Jesus said: Don't spoil your soul by worrying about another man's salvation. He did not mean we should not care for one another, but that we should refrain from jealous comparisons. Then again came the call: Follow me! Jesus was telling Peter that He had a way for each of His followers and that each way might be different—but nonetheless part of God's plan.

JESUS ANSWERS THE QUESTION OF THE KINGDOM

The occasion is recorded in the Book of Acts and in Luke's account of the days after His death. These were the days, Luke tells us, when Jesus spoke to his Disciples about "... the things pertaining to the kingdom of God: ..." The place of the meeting was evidently near Bethany on the hillside where they had often met.

The question was direct: "... Lord, wilt thou at this time restore again the kingdom to Israel?" The Disciples assumed Jesus would bring the purpose of God to final consummation and would restore the Kingdom to Israel.

Jesus answered this question along three lines: a correction, a promise, and a commission.

First, he said it was not for them to know the times or seasons of God. He rebuked their curiosity and taught them that His Disciples had nothing to do with predicting the times and dates of God's intervention.

Second, he promised them power through the Holy Spirit. This was to be the inward power of His presence and the coming of the Spirit into their lives.

Third, He called them to be witnesses to God's truth throughout the world, witnesses to God's Kingdom.

THE ANSWERS OF JESUS TO SAUL

The questions and answers of the Risen Lord are found in the great hour of the conversion of Saul of Tarsus, who later became Paul. The account is found in the Book of Acts.

Through three sections in the Book of Acts, we are given the full account. The first is the record of Luke of the conversion of Saul in Chapter 9. The second is the account of Paul's own rehearsal of the conversion in Chapter 22. And the third is the account of Paul's conversion before King Agrippa in Chapter 26.

Saul was a Hebrew born of Jewish parents in Cilicia, the second educational center of the world, the heart of Greek culture. Yet Paul also was a Roman citizen. All these elements merged in his personality. Taught by Gamaliel, he also was a member of the Sanhedrin. Beyond all this, he was violently opposed to Jesus. Our introduction to Saul is that of his voting for the stoning of the Christian martyr, Stephen.

Saul was on his way to Damascus, bringing with him letters to the high priest, so that he might find followers of Jesus and bring them bound to Jerusalem. Saul and his travelers reached the hilltop over Damascus when suddenly the crisis came. From the heavens flashed a blinding light and a voice spoke "... Saul, Saul, why persecutest thou me? ..."

The light and voice, which Paul later called the heavenly vision, broke upon him. He was absolutely certain it was Jesus. "... I looked up upon him." was his assured conviction.

Saul asked two questions. Who art thou Lord? What shall I do, Lord?

The first answer of Jesus is a revelation in itself: "I am Jesus of Nazareth, whom thou persecutest." Up to this moment, Jesus had been a dead man, disgraced, and unholy. But here, on the road, Jesus identified Himself with all those who were persecuted. Through them, He was being persecuted.

The second answer of Jesus to Saul was a command: "... Arise, and go into Damascus, and there it shall be told thee of all things which are appointed for thee to do." This is always the Master's plan: one step at a time. It was a difficult thing for Saul to do. Those who loved Jesus expected him as a great enemy. Now he must come as a Disciple.

The first answer of Jesus to Saul reveals the fact of His constant pursuit of every one of us. He is always pursuing. Whether in great sorrow or moments of great crisis, it is God who is approaching your soul. The second answer of Jesus is a revelation of His guidance for us daily. Follow His leading one step at a time, and it shall be revealed what to do next.

JESUS RESPONDS ABOUT THE END OF THE WORLD

Among our Lord's answers to questions of His own Disciples there is recorded one memorable hour, when they asked Him some questions about a constantly recurring subject for all Christians: When will He come again? This is certainly a question of believers in times of social upheaval and world calamity.

It is His answer—and not human teaching—that is the basis of our consideration. Two schools of thought need to be avoided when dealing with this subject. First is the thought of those who dismiss the teachings about the end of the world and who are embarrassed by what Jesus had to say. Second are the thoughts of those literalists who have mapped out on their own the exact moment of the Second Coming and who think those not subscribing to this belief are agnostics.

It was Tuesday of His last week before the cross. He had made his triumphal entry into Jerusalem. Early on Monday on His way back to Jerusalem He had destroyed the fig tree and cleansed the Temple. But on Tuesday He entered into conflict with the rulers. At the close of the day, He sat and watched the givers in the treasury and praised the gift of the poor widow. Immediately after this His Disciples drew His attention to the beauty of the buildings and the stones. Jesus then predicted the destruction of the Temple. Leaving this building, He then came to a place on a mountainside overlooking the Temple.

Four Disciples—Peter, James, John, and Andrew—asked him privately: "... Tell us, when shall these things be? and what shall be the sign of thy coming, and of the end of the world?" "These things" was a reference to the destruction of the Temple. "Thy coming" was associated with the judgment. "End of the world" should actually be translated as the "consummation of the age." From His teaching they would have deduced that one age came to its consummation with His birth. This reference was to the Second Coming.

The answer of Jesus to these questions is one of the longest ever coming from His lips. In Matthew, it occupies all of Chapters 24 and 25. Throughout His answer there is the clear prediction that human history moves to a climax, where the reign of God shall become a reality, on earth as it is in heaven.

Three principles can be derived from these teachings of Jesus about the end: (1) From the cross to the consummation there would be perpetual conflict; (2) Wars and rumors of wars are not the signs of the end of the world; and (3) There are solemn warnings about false leaders and messiahs. Implicit also in His teachings are two declarations about the end. First, the approach of the end will be marked by supernatural signs in nature and in history. Second, no one knows for certain when the end will come.

THE ANSWERS OF JESUS TO THE QUESTIONS OF EVIL

In the study of the religions of the world there is perhaps nothing more startling than the discovery of the universal belief in the existence of evil. The New Testament recognizes evil forces and gives very definite teachings about the opposition of evil to God's purpose. The testimony of the Gospels is unequivocal as to the existence of Satan and demons. Not once, but again and again, we read of the warnings of Jesus about the dark forces of evil. It is true that some dismiss the notion of Satan by claiming that Jesus did not really know what was behind evil or that His thoughts were pre-scientific. But, we must examine the reality of the New Testament, for it affirmed the existence of an arch enemy, his access to human history, and the harm wrought in life by the workings of evil.

Jesus spoke of evil under three names: Satan, the adversary; the Devil, the false accuser; and Beelzebub, the master of the dung hill. Describing the work of Satan, John says he was a "... murderer from the beginning, and abode not in the truth, because there is no truth in him."

Whatever we think about the New Testament teaching concerning evil, it is obvious that the fact of evil is manifest everywhere in our world. The mystery of iniquity is an abiding one, and we face it anew in each generation. We look at the horrifying depths of evil in the human heart: its self-centered ambitions, calculating greed, nauseating self-interests of politics, and the cynical treacheries of international policies—all that Paul had in mind when he wrote that evil holds "... [down] the truth in unrighteousness." We live in a world that professes the dignity of mankind and, then, proceeds to blow each other to pieces.

Jesus faced the reality of evil directly and not as an intellectual problem. Two occasions in the New Testament record times when the voices of evil asked Jesus questions.

In Mark 1:24 and Luke 4:34 there is one question: "what have we to do with thee, thou Jesus of Nazareth? ... I know thee who thou art; the Holy One of God." It was the cry of a man possessed with an evil spirit, speaking in the synagogue on the Sabbath. In Matthew 8:29, Mark 5:7, and Luke 8:28, we find another question: "What have I to do with thee, Jesus, *thou* son of the most high God? I adjure thee by God, that thou torment me not." It was the cry of a man possessed by demons.

Jesus, in both cases reported above, responded with only a few words: "... Come out of the man, thou unclean spirit." There was no discussion, no compromise with evil. There was a recognition of its power and a word of authority to cast it out.

The questions of the evil spirits are a revelation of their methods. Though evil forces say they do not believe in the power of God, they constantly seek to get rid of God. And, when confronted with the goodness of God, they offer a subtle plea for compromise, for appeasement in the moral and spiritual realm. They want to be left alone.

But Jesus did not compromise. He answered, not by retreating mildly and meekly, but by the expulsion of the dark forces. In this way, we should understand that through Jesus we, too, have resources for the triumph of goodness over evil. Through His strength we can be more than conquerors over the dark powers and principalities of the world.

IV

A NEW MAN
IN CHRIST

Of all the persons who came to Jesus, perhaps none is more familiar than Simon Peter. He often seemed the largest in human scale among the Twelve Disciples. He represents, as well, not only the heights of human experience, but also the lowest moments. In short, he still holds our attention, as much for his humanity as his faith, after all these centuries. By a careful study of the life of Simon Peter, we come to an understanding of the human dimension—of what it means to be under the power of the Risen Lord. Simon, who denied Jesus, becomes "the rock." In this simple, yet sublime development, it is possible to see the workings of the Holy Spirit upon the personality of a human being.

There are two great hours of crisis to which we must return in thinking about Simon Peter. Two texts serve as the focal points of study. The first is the declaration of Jesus about the faith of Simon Peter. The second is Peter's response to Jesus.

In Matthew 16:18, we read: "And I say also unto thee, That thou art Peter, and upon this rock I will build my church." In this statement, Jesus indicated that he knew Peter's weaknesses but was confident of his possibilities. Like a rock, Peter was to be made slowly by heat, by pressure, and by upheaval.

And then we have a record of the great confession of Peter: "Thou art the Christ, the Son of the living God." And this is followed by the benediction of Jesus: "... upon this rock I will build ..." What is this rock? It is Jesus Himself, the experience of God in Christ. In the person of the changed Simon, we are confronted with the reality of God moving in the human personality, taking the clay of existence and making a new man.

DENYING THE CHRIST

All four Gospels tell the story of Peter's denial of Jesus. Each of the Evangelists writes the story with simplicity and graphic power. It is significant to remember that Mark wrote the story in its entirety, perhaps hearing it from the lips of Peter himself. Peter did not hide his shame; he permitted it to be part of the Gospel record. There is no cover-up here and no hiding of facts. Surely Peter must have meant the story to be told as a warning and as an encouragement to all those who deny Jesus and later follow Him. Perhaps our fascination with Peter is that he allowed himself to be transparent before us, not as a marble saint but as a real man, fearful of the Gospel and caught in his own despair.

In Luke, Chapter 22, Verses 31 through 34 and Verses 54 through 62, we have the story of Peter and Jesus. Luke provides unique touches not found in the other Evangelists' records. It is Luke who writes that "... the Lord turned, and looked upon Peter. ..." who stood in the courtyard denying Him.

What preceded the denial of Peter? Jesus had told Peter that he was in danger of being overcome by evil. Peter had denied this, telling Jesus he would not deny Him. But Jesus had responded: "... the cock shall not crow this day, before that thou shalt thrice deny that thou knowest me." The Gospel records show that Peter did deny Jesus, but there was a previous history of denials. On at least six other occasions, Peter denied Jesus. He questioned Jesus about the need for the cross. He was a rebel against the notion of sacrifice. He boasted in pride that he would never deny his Master. He denied Jesus when he could not pray with Him at the Garden of Gethsemane. He took out a sword to protect Jesus, thus denying His path of peace. He often fell behind his Master in crucial hours.

The denials of Peter are also our denials. We decline to follow Jesus out of fear. We boast about our faith, but inside we are full of anxiety. We fail to follow Jesus with our prayers; when He truly needs us, we fall asleep. We have zeal about our beliefs but do not truly understand the Gospel. We follow Jesus from afar.

But what is important to remember is that Jesus never denied Peter—no matter how frail and weak he might have become. He loved Peter. He prayed for Peter. Because Jesus knew Peter, knew his strengths and his weaknesses, He never gave him up as lost. Nothing separates us from the love of God, not even our own denials.

SEEING CHRIST'S GLORY

In the story of Peter, we find one of the most fascinating biographies in the New Testament. Impulsive, full of failures, but struck with faith, Simon Peter was chosen by Jesus as one of the early Christian leaders. The study of Peter's life is in many respects a study of the principal events of the Gospel narrative, especially as the Good News works as a transforming reality in the life of one human being.

Perhaps no event in the life of Peter stayed with him as long as the transfiguration of Jesus. Peter himself wrote: "For we have not followed cunningly devised fables, when we made known unto you the power and coming of our Lord Jesus Christ, but were eyewitnesses of his majesty. For he received from God the Father honour and glory, when there came such a voice to him from the excellent glory, This is my beloved Son, in whom I am well pleased. And this voice which came from heaven we heard, when we were with him in the holy mount." (II Peter 1:16-18)

All three of the synoptic Gospels record the event of the transfiguration of Jesus. It is important to note carefully the time of its occurrence. The event is recorded as taking place "... after six days ..." The logical question is: Six days after what? The answer is six days after Jesus had announced His cross to the Disciples.

In order to understand what the transfiguration of Jesus meant to Peter, his experience can be broken into four categories: (1) what Peter saw, (2) what Peter said, (3) what Peter heard, and (4) what Peter learned.

Peter saw His Master at prayer on a high mountain. Suddenly, Christ's face shone and His garments became white with a dazzling light. And, with Jesus, there were two men, Moses and Elias. This transfiguration experience was the consummation of His human life, the natural culmination of all that He had taught and done. He could have, at that moment, entered the heavenly realm without tasting death. It was this glory that confronted Peter, this beatific vision.

What Peter said may be seen as a perfectly normal reaction for a fisherman. "... Lord, it is good for us to be here: if thou wilt, let us make here three tabernacles; one for thee, and one for Moses, and one for Elias."

What Peter heard, even as he made this proposal, was a voice from heaven, declaring: "... This is my beloved Son, in whom I am well pleased; ..."

What Peter learned from the experience was that the cross of Jesus was His supreme sacrifice given as a ransom for many. Jesus did not bypass the human event of death; He entered willingly into the valley of the shadow of death. This is the glory of Christ that He emptied Himself, even unto death.

A DECLARATION FOR JESUS

In John 21:15, we read: "So when they had dined, Jesus saith to Simon Peter, Simon, son of Jonas, lovest thou me more than these? He saith unto him, Yea, Lord; thou knowest that I love thee."

In the life of Peter this early morning experience with the Risen Christ would stand out forever in his mind. It is one of the great epochs of the story of this fisherman.

There are, nonetheless, contrasts and similarities in this story. Peter had denied his Master in the city. But now the hour is away from the city and by the sea. Peter had denied his Master by night, but now it is early morning. Peter had denied his Master by a fire built by His enemies, but now it is with holy fire that he declares his love.

The first call to Peter had been "... follow me ..." and now the last call is the same, "... Follow me." Peter had denied his Lord; now he affirms his love.

Every time I read this passage I wonder why the question was asked of Peter three times: Lovest thou Me? Some would say because Peter also had denied Jesus three times. But I wonder if this captures the full impact of the message. Could it not be that Jesus was stressing the importance of Peter's declaration? One is reminded here of the passage from Ecclesiastes: "... a threefold cord is not quickly broken."

Jesus asked Peter a question three times. The occasion was an informal breakfast and not a formal hearing. The Risen Lord had built a fire and prepared breakfast. He made the Disciples sit down, and He waited upon them. Jesus was leading Peter from a simple declaration of friendship to a love of great emotion and admiring affection.

As a result of this declaration, Jesus gave Peter a threefold commission. The first was to give spiritual and physical sustenance to the people, most especially those in greatest need. The second was to guard the community of the faithful against the onslaught of wolves who would scatter the sheep. And the third was to provide spiritual sustenance to those who hunger after God.

PROCLAIMING THE CHRIST

Simon Peter preaches the first Christian sermon in the history of the church. It is a great epoch in the beginning of the church, as it is a great proclamation for Jesus. The Second Chapter of the Book of Acts should be known, read, and digested by every student of the Bible. It is one of the most important pages of church history, for it outlines the basic principles of Christian belief and practice.

A summary of the chapter needs to be given, though our special interest is in Peter. The Second Chapter can be briefly summarized as follows:
1. The coming of the Holy Spirit (1-4).
2. The confounded multitudes (5-13).
3. The Christian sermon (14-36).
4. The conscience-stricken hearers (37-41).
5. The normal life of the church (42-47).

The immediate reason for Peter's sermon was that the people were confused. They were also critical, claiming that the believers were "drunk."

Peter's sermon can be divided into four sections.
1. The Introduction (14-21): Here Peter makes reference to the life of the Disciples, citing revelations of old prophets and refuting the idea of drunkenness.
2. The Proclamation (22-36): Peter evokes the name of Jesus, who has demonstrated perfection as a "... man approved of God among you by

miracles and wonders and signs, ..." He then proceeds to describe the crucifixion of Jesus at the hands of lawless men and His resurrection, where He was exalted by God. Jesus is then received by God, who pours forth His Holy Spirit.

3. The Invitation (37-43): Peter then issues the invitation to "Repent, and be baptized every one of you in the name of Jesus Christ ..."

4. The Exhortation (40): Here Peter tells the people to save themselves "from this untoward generation."

The sermon concludes with the statement that the people continue steadfastly in the teaching of the Apostles, in fellowship, and in prayer and the breaking of bread.

A GOOD MANNER OF LIFE IN CHRIST

The first letter in Peter's teachings are a result of his being transformed by the power of Jesus. His major theme is that of the Christian pilgrim.

The first statements of Peter's letter are typical of his faith. He talks about a living hope, of being a pilgrim in all aspects of life: political, social, domestic, and personal.

Peter then describes the qualities of a true Christian: like-minded, sympathetic, loving, humble, and blessed. He sees these qualities as marks of the "good life" in Christ. But, Peter also sees suffering as the pathway of love. To suffer for goodness is better than prospering for evil, simply because Jesus suffered for the sake of humanity.

POWER WHICH IS NOT PURCHASABLE

Peter and John are on the open road; they are in Samaria. How remarkable this is, considering the fact that the prejudice of the time was against Samaritans. The central scene is about Christianity's first encounter with superstition and also a subtle form of commercialism.

Following the martyrdom of Stephen, the Disciples were scattered. During one of the trips, Simon Peter met Simon the Magnus, who was a sorcerer. This magician tried to offer Simon Peter money in order to receive the power of the Holy Spirit. Simon Peter's response was quick and to the point: "Thy money perish with thee, ..." He allowed no compromise.

The danger faced here by Simon Peter has continued to be one facing Christians throughout the ages: the treatment of spiritual functions as a marketable commodity. Money can buy diamonds but not wisdom, sympathy, faith, nor holiness. Simon Peter refused to use religion as a means of personal aggrandizement. His power was not for purchase. The power of Jesus comes as a gift to those who are obedient.

CHAPTER

V

THE POWER OF CHRIST
FOR HUMAN PROBLEMS

Not every one that saith unto me, Lord, Lord, shall enter into
the kingdom of heaven; but he that doeth the will of my
Father which is in heaven.
(Matthew 7:21)

... If any *man* will come after me, let him deny himself, and take
up his cross, and follow me.
(Matthew 16:24)

For whosoever will save his life shall lose it: and whosoever
will lose his life for my sake shall find it.
(Matthew 16:25)

These three passages from the Gospel of Matthew are self-evident
warnings of Jesus about the depth of the human problem. These three
passages are words spoken by Jesus to His Disciples on two prominent
occasions in His ministry. The first saying was uttered at the close of the
Sermon on the Mount. The second two sayings were spoken at Caesarea
Philippi, when He first announced His cross to His followers.

But what is the deadly sin of humanity, the depth of the human problem? One is reminded here of the classic story of the Holy Grail and the
Round Table, especially the epic of Sir Galahad, the knightly prince,
"whose strength was as the strength of ten because his heart was pure."
Sir Galahad battled against the Seven Deadly Sins, which have been vari-
ously described as murder, theft, indulgence, pride, greed, selfishness,
and godlessness. Rev. Canon Frederic Lewis Donaldson of Westminster
Abbey has reinterpreted these seven deadly sins in more modern terms,
and these seem to strike at the heart of the human problem. These
updated sins are:
1. Policies without principles.
2. Wealth without work.
3. Pleasure without conscience.
4. Knowledge without character.
5. Industry without morality.

6. Science without humanity.
7. Worship without sacrifice.

POLICY WITHOUT PRINCIPLE

Ours is genuinely a time of despair and doubt, but these are qualities of being not entirely common to this century. But the depth of evil in our time and the powers of destruction before us should not blind us to the tightrope of existence upon which we walk. Policy without principle in our age can doom us to extinction.

A group of students once declared there were five conditions under which a lie was justified: (1) It is right to lie in politics; (2) It is right to lie in business; (3) It is right to lie to save a life; (4) It is right to lie to support a noble cause; and (5) It is right to lie during war.

There are in these five declarations clear conflicts between policies and principles. A classical illustration from the New Testament sets in sharper focus the dimension of the conflicts. When facing Jesus, Pilate turned Him over to be crucified; policy dictated a compromise and a cruci-fixion—even though Pilate knew in his heart that Jesus was not guilty. Here, in this case, policy won over principle.

But Jesus never placed policy before principle. If He had done so, then God would have been a liar, unable to be trusted. In response to the students, Jesus might have responded:

1. A lie in politics breaks the confidence of character; it is the danger-ous enemy of national life.

2. A lie in business builds upon sand; sooner or later the lie breaks against the moral fiber of the universe.

3. A lie to save a life breaks the element of trust and confidence, thus killing character, which is the basis of life.

4. A lie to serve a noble cause is impossible because the cause is then made imperfect. The means never justify the ends.

5. A lie in war simply justifies the evil of war itself and turns war into something noble and self-righteous.

WEALTH WITHOUT WORK

This is a generation that has swallowed the notion of possessions with a wild passion and believes the measure of a person is his or her accumula-tions. It is also a generation that believes in wealth without work.

Wealth, legitimately acquired and honestly shared, is not a sin. Jesus did not condemn a person for being rich. Only the individual who ac-quired wealth without stewardship to God and to other human beings was condemned. There is a Gospel for the rich as well as the poor; in fact, it must be remembered that often rich persons can be as "poor in spirit" as the poorest individuals.

There are clear teachings of Jesus about wealth. In the Sermon on the Mount, He tells people not to lay up for themselves treasures on earth, "But lay up for yourselves treasures in heaven, ..." The principle affirmed here is found in the word *yourselves*. Selfish consumption and the accumulation of possessions become gods unto themselves and not for the sake of others.

Again, in the Parable of the Rich Fool (Luke 12:13-23), the story is told of a man who wanted Jesus to divide up some property. Jesus concluded the parable by saying that the Rich Fool laid up treasure for himself but was not rich toward God. Wealth by itself is no sin, but far too many wealthy fail to share their wealth with others.

Jesus certainly never indicated that wealth would bring happiness; on the contrary, He often said that the pursuit of wealth for its own sake was a stumbling block to faith. His most harsh criticisms were often directed against those who were given much but refused to share what they had with the poor. And, more importantly, it was His acts that set the tone for the principle. He never accumulated wealth. He worked as a common laborer. He became one with the poor in spirit. He turned His back on the kingdoms of this world.

PLEASURE WITHOUT CONSCIENCE

Pleasure without conscience is one of the deadly perils of this generation. In the Declaration of Independence, one finds the goal of the "pursuit of happiness." The Christian faith, contrary to what some may believe, is not opposed to happiness. There is in Jesus a quality of joy, but it is not the carefree pleasure of persons swishing about the trough, taking whatever they can for the pleasure of the moment.

It is important to recall the words of Jesus about joy, or pleasure with conscience. One needs only remember His words in the Sermon on the Mount that describe the quality of life of those who believe in Him: blessed, prosperous, and happy. Every beatitude rings with true happiness. Recall also many of His parables, ending on notes of joy. The joy is not pleasure taken without conscience but the happiness of recovery and of finding life after so much death!

What must be considered is the difference between the joy of Jesus and that of the world. Jesus taught that persons are more than flesh; therefore, true pleasures must be higher than appeasement of the animal, physical appetite. It is not that physical pleasure is not important—far from it. Physical pleasure is part of God's creation, but apart from mental and spiritual pleasure is a perversion of God's love for us.

What kinds of joy did Jesus describe?

First, he talked about the joy of communion with God. This joy is rooted in loving life, because God is the giver of life.

Second, Jesus never talked about solitary pleasure, but the joy in lifting other lives and in relating to others. The mark of our age is one of seeking self-fulfillment. But what is the self if not a complex series of relationships to others? And if the self is related to God, the ultimate source of our being, what greater joy can a human being imagine?

Third, Jesus talked about the joy of sacrifice. It was not enough to find happiness at the expense of others. Rather, true joy was to be found in our taking the part of the other person, not losing ourselves but rather enriching ourselves through the encounter.

KNOWLEDGE WITHOUT CHARACTER

> And it came to pass, when Jesus had ended these sayings, the people were astonished at his doctrine: For he taught them as *one* having authority, and not as the scribes.
>
> (Matthew 7:28-29)
>
> And the whole multitude sought to touch him: For there went virtue out of him, and healed *them* all.
>
> (Luke 6:19)

These words were written by Matthew and Luke. In Matthew the words are from the Sermon on the Mount; in Luke, the words introduce the sayings of Jesus.

There is a deadly peril of knowledge without character set loose in our times. The texts cited refer to the authority of Jesus and His power. In Luke, the reference refers to Christ's power to heal disease, but it is also valid for His power to cure the moral maladies of human hearts.

The Sermon on the Mount, and especially the Beatitudes, reveal the teachings of Jesus about knowledge with character. It is His clear counsel that knowledge, apart from character, is incomplete—indeed, it can become destructive.

It is vital that we remember that Jesus did not pronounce blessings on persons for what they possessed nor for what they had done, but rather for their inwardness. He spoke of the poor in spirit, the meek, those that hunger after righteousness, and the peacemakers. He said the pure in heart would see God and through the creation of a new being would form new characters. This inward enrichment of the spirit is the path to knowledge.

Our age, trained intellectually, has already approached the beginning of its own end. It is thought that because of our scientific advancement we are on the verge of a new human condition, without considering that very little has changed in the heart of mankind since Jesus walked on earth. In fact, it may well be that our material achievements have outdistanced our social wisdom, so spiritually we are confused and often lost. Superfluous ideas abound, but essential ideas are missing. Remember the story of the son of Louis XIV, who had his son trained by two great professors. With all this intellectual learning, it was written that the son "was fond of killing weasels." Intellectual advancement without character may simply turn destructive.

One of the more persuasive "religions" of our day is the one that teaches that God has disappeared from history. The universe seems dead and totally indifferent to values. Our lives, therefore, are without final purpose or meaning except that meaning which we appropriate for ourselves, often at the expense of others.

Over against this contemporary view one must place the life and teachings of Jesus. There is God's purpose in the world; the universe is not indifferent to our deepest values. Humanity has not been abandoned because the heart of God is like a father who cares for our spirits and bodies and wants us to inherit His Kingdom. The power of Jesus creates character, knowledge, and faith so that we may become co-creators under God of a new order.

INDUSTRY WITHOUT MORALITY

> For what shall it profit a man, if he shall gain the whole world, and lose his own soul?
>
> (Mark 8:36)

This summoning and searching question of Jesus is one response to the issue of industry without morality. Perhaps it would be more illuminating to describe Christ's summons to spirituality in industry, for in this way we do justice to industry rightly conceived—and to the power of Jesus over the meaning of human labor.

The word "spiritually" here means the values of the spirit of man in his relationship to God and to his neighbors—in other words, his morality. We know what the word morality means in a Christian sense, but actually the word comes from the French word, moris, meaning manners or customs. Jesus calls for more than conformance to customs, for one may confuse doing what is customary for what is right.

Work is one of the first laws of human history, according to the Biblical record. Work is one of those essential qualities that governs human existence. Jesus reinforced this truth in the Sermon on the Mount when he recognized the power to work as a special gift which raises human beings above the levels of other animals. He recognizes all callings and gifts as realities from God. Paul also is clear in his exposition of this truth when he writes to the Thessalonians that "... if any would not work, neither should he eat." To the Ephesians he writes that work is not only for one's own support but "... that he may have to give to him that needeth."

Work is made important, therefore, to all persons and for all persons, provided the fruits of labor are shared.

It is interesting to discover the meaning of work among the words of the writer of the Egyptian Book of the Dead, which is found in the tomb of an Egyptian princess. She drives a pair of cream-colored cows to a plow, cracking her whip across their backs. She cuts a luxuriant field of wheat, taller than her head, with a golden sickle. She paddles a green canoe on the lakes of Elysium. Finally, she guards a pile of yellow grain for her master, Osiris. Work, work, always work—this was her chief joy.

The summons of Jesus is that we bring spirituality to bear upon our industry. The Golden Rule is applicable to work, for without its principle both managers and workers grow mistrustful and alienated. Jesus would have us be stewards over our labor, understanding that work is divinely proposed. No follower of Jesus can amass a fortune simply to accumulate possessions. No follower of Jesus can oppress his workers. No Christian, in short, can be a follower of Jesus if he or she does not take God into the marketplace and call Him Lord of all life.

SCIENCE WITHOUT HUMANITY

There is in modern times a diabolic chain of events set loose when science without humanity gains control. The faith of our time seems to be that science will save us—from what, if not ourselves? But science, as labor, is part of God's creation and meant to be understood rightly.

Just as we are to become stewards for God over the world of work, so, too, should we become stewards of our science for God's Kingdom. If our science becomes destructive, if it threatens the very existence of humanity, it is no longer either a science nor a force for human improvement.

Science, rightly conceived in Christian terms, is a gift from God. If science enables us to feed the hungry or clothe the poor, it is rooted in Christian values. If it opens up new dimensions of God's universe, it partakes of the mystery of creation.

WORSHIP WITHOUT SACRIFICE

Sacrifice is the very heart of religion. The first chapter of the Christian story has been written about the sacrifice of God through His Son. We cannot go one step with Him without hearing the unavoidable challenge that we are to lay down our lives for the brethren. "... If any *man* will come after me, let him deny himself, and take up his cross, and follow me."

It is shameful to admit that the prejudices against Christianity are often rooted in our inability to live the meaning of the Gospel. We can understand how a thoughtful observer might conclude that our worship is without sacrifice or that we have watered down the Good News to fit our need for comfort. Worship has often been reduced to a cheap manner of escape so that we might well be called the Church of the Heavenly Rest.

Jesus sought to take human beings away from petty and secure values into the unknown sea of living. He cast us into the world as His Disciples, giving us His strength to continue the good fight.

The Christian Gospel is everywhere a Gospel of vicarious sacrifice—a love that suffers and a life that gives itself for others. It centers upon Calvary and radiates from that hill. Somehow, the extended arms of Jesus on the cross embrace the whole world, taking in all manner of life. As His Disciples, we are called to radiate His love, to minister to others, to pour out our lives in sunlight and the deepest darkness, and to be His witnesses to the end of this world—for which He gave His own life in the supreme sacrifice of universal history.

CHAPTER

VI

ETERNAL ANSWERS TO MODERN QUESTIONS

IS CONVERSION OUT OF DATE?

> And said, Verily I say unto you, Except ye be converted, and become as little children, ye shall not enter into the kingdom of heaven.
>
> (Matthew 18:3)
>
> Let him know, that he which converteth the sinner from the error of his way shall save a soul from death, and shall hide a multitude of sins.
>
> (James 5:20)

Is conversion out of date?

This is a question that is often heard by ministers in the Twentieth Century, although conversion may appear to be a relic from a past century. It is a question that deserves an honest response.

What is conversion? Some believe it is a dizzy, emotional experience. This kind of experience sounds much like a man on a trampoline— jumping up and down he always ends up just where he started.

Conversion means a change and a lasting change at that. Recall the two scriptural passages cited above. In Matthew we read the great words of Jesus about conversion and about the turning away from pride and self-conceit to humility and confidence. Again, in the passage of James, we read that conversion is necessary for faith.

A change of thought and behavior is frequently vital to mental health. If a person is haunted by bleak loneliness and tries to escape from it through alcohol or drugs, the only pathway out is making new plans and ways of thinking to help conquer depression. If, on the other hand, a person suffers a great loss such as the death of a loved one, the way of rescue lies in a new motive for living—a restructuring of patterns of behavior.

Many of us are weak in character because we are split personalities. We serve too many masters. For this reason, we often feel as if we muddle through life, literally sailing in circles. We need a change to refocus our sense of purpose and direction and enable us to concentrate on what is truly ultimate. We need a conversion of our thoughts and behavior.

How does conversion come? Sometimes it is preceded by periods of great doubt and despair. Reaching the point of some deep abyss, we look elsewhere other than to our normal reactions. In looking, we may find a new set of ideas or person. Paul looks into the radiant face of Jesus and changes. Levi, the tax collector, peers into the face of Jesus and follows Him.

Conversion requires some degree of receptivity. It is a relationship. If we hear a knock at the door and never answer it, we do not know what is beyond the knock. Conversion also depends upon power coming to us from outside. We may be so caught in our own despair that we lack the personal resources to overcome our sickness. But, then, the power of God enters our life and creates a new direction.

WHAT IS LOSING LIFE TO FIND IT?

> For whosoever will save his life shall lose it: and whosoever will lose his life for my sake shall find it.
>> (Matthew 16:25)

> He that findeth his life shall lose it: and he that loseth his life for my sake shall find it.
>> (Matthew 10:39)

> Whosoever shall seek to save his life shall lose it; and whosoever shall lose his life shall preserve it.
>> (Luke 17:33)

Three times in the Gospels the words of Jesus are recorded about losing life in order to find it. First, at Caesarea Philippi, the words are used by Jesus to describe His own death and the meaning of the cross for His Disciples. After explicitly affirming His suffering and death on the cross—and being doubted by Peter—Jesus responds that His Disciples must take up His cross in order to follow Him.

The second time Jesus refers to losing life comes at the hour when He commissions The Twelve and gives them instructions about their mission. He speaks of the cost of discipleship in stern terms: "I came not to send peace but a sword. ..."

The third time Jesus was speaking to His Disciples about the great calamities that come about in the world.

In all three cases, Jesus was not speaking of physical life, but of the essential life of the spirit—the center and core of personality. He was stating a great law of human psychology. He is not commanding the mutilation of personality, but rather calling persons to abandon their crippling egomania in order to gain a larger view of life.

Consider today the broken spirits of humanity; think of the hidden despair and anxiety. Our personalities are literally divided. We are not so much beside ourselves as imprisoned within.

In the midst of this internal struggle, Jesus calls out for us to give up and follow Him. We must deny ourselves, meaning that part of our personality that seeks to affirm itself without thought of others. And, in denying that boastful part of ourselves, we enter into His Kingdom, which is to say into a deeper relationship with God and His creation.

IS THERE ANYTHING IN PRAYING FOR OTHERS?

> I pray for them: ...
>
> (John 17:9)
>
> Neither pray I these alone, but for them also which shall believe on me through their word;
>
> (John 17:20)

Why do people, devout people, mistrust prayer or feel it is not necessary?

Some say prayer is useless because everything is fated. They throw up their hands with the expectation that everything will work out, one way or another. It is interesting to note, however, that they apply this knowledge to others rather than themselves. If they would see a bomb dropping out of the sky, they would not stand still waiting for fate to take its course. No, they would run rapidly and utter a simple, but quick prayer.

Others would say that prayer is unnecessary because God already has all in His care and does not need our reminders. This may be true for the first part of the statement, for God does have all in His care. But if He does not need our reminders, we need to remind ourselves that He is a loving source of strength.

In the Gospels there is the story of the crippled man who had to be carried to Jesus to be healed. In prayer we can do the same for our friends, if not physically then certainly spiritually. In praying for them, we are lifting them to Jesus; we are channels along which God's power is transmitted.

While most are prone to think of prayer as an individual act, it is important to note that it also is a social experience. We do not pray to ourselves alone but to God, and this is a relationship. Moreover, we also pray for others, and this involves a social network. So, even when we go into our rooms to pray alone, we are not alone. The act of prayer lifts us from the purely solitary into the spiritually interpersonal.

The New Testament, moreover, does provide some guidance in praying for others.

First, our prayers should be definite. We need to visualize the persons about whom and for whom we pray; we need to set a picture of Jesus in our minds as we think of our friends—or our enemies.

Second, prayer is not a once-and-for-all event, but rather a continuous process that is part of our own spiritual growth. Keep on praying!

Third, prayer requires submission—the very act of which hurts our pride. We must come in reverent recognition of God's wisdom and power.

God does answer prayers for others. He does not always respond to our own requests nor answer our prayers in the way we hoped. But there is always a response. So let us pray for others.

WHY DOES BELIEF MATTER?

> And if it seem evil unto you to serve the Lord, choose you this day whom ye will serve; whether the gods which your fathers served that *were* on the other side of the Flood, or the gods of the Amorites, in whose land ye dwell: but as for me and my house, we will serve the Lord.
>
> (Joshua 24:15)
>
> ... Thou shalt worship the Lord thy God, and him only shalt thou serve.
>
> (Matthew 4:10)

The question about whether belief is important is both an ancient and modern one. Every generation asks this question sooner or later, in one form or another.

The question itself may be asked from two distinct viewpoints. There are those who have a contempt for all belief, feeling it to be worthless and antiquated. They do not want an honest answer, for they feel that faith does not matter except in a destructive way. The question also may be asked by those who do not feel that morality depends upon any relationship with a creed. They are not sure of the answer but are at least willing to listen.

In the Book of Joshua, we have this old challenge issued to the nation by its leader. In a farewell address to his nation, Joshua had traced the course of their history. The necessity for religion is stressed: "... choose you this day whom ye will serve; ..." It might appear from this that had the people rejected God, then the question of belief might be left out. But no, Joshua continued, if not the god of your fathers, then what god? Human life is so constructed that the question of belief cannot be dismissed entirely, for it represents a center of values and devotion. Whatever the protest—even rebellion against God—there is a core of belief; whatever is considered of ultimate value is a faith, even if it does not go by the name.

In the Gospel of Matthew, Jesus responds to the presence of evil with this direct declaration: "Thou shalt worship the Lord thy God, and him only shalt thou serve." This is the important principle of faith. Whatever we worship as the center of life is our god, and we give ourselves over in service. Every person serves some inner shrine or god, some ultimate set of values.

Belief does matter. If I believe that life is meaningless, I may act out this belief in practice. G.K. Chesterton used to say that if he were looking for lodgings, he might ask his landlord about his total view of the universe, for this would tell him whether the sheets would be clean and the rent fair!

Beliefs matter socially as well. If pleasure is our true value, then selfishness is the social order, for each person would then pursue his or her happiness no matter what the costs. If we believe that life is simply a biological struggle, then our society may reflect intense competition. Or, if we believe with Jesus that life has great value, then our society may promote environments of mutual respect and cooperation.

WHY ARE GOOD PEOPLE SO OFTEN AGGRAVATING?

But woe unto you, scribes and Pharisees, hypocrites! ...
(Matthew 23:13)
Judge not, that ye be not judged. ...Thou hypocrite, first cast out the beam out of thine own eye; ...
(Matthew 7:1 and 7:5)

Why are good people so often aggravating?

The questioner was asking what he thought to be a fair question. He could not understand why the outwardly pious seemed so insistent on forcing their views down his throat and so intolerant of other opinions. In short, he concluded that often "good people" seemed to him to be dull, petty, and narrow. One is reminded here of the essay written by a young school girl about Queen Victoria, who took as her coronation motto, "I will be good." The young student wrote in her essay that Queen Victoria had lived "a long and *tedious* life."

There are good people whose lives are scant of adventure. There are conservative Christians who want things done as they have always been done. They dislike change, mistrust new ideas, and seem shut off from life itself. There are other pious persons who are narrow and bitter. They are always condemning others. They are concerned about little things and lax about ultimate things.

Jesus certainly encountered a number of "good people" in his public ministry; those for whom the ultimate questions of existence consisted in debating what color the altar cloth must be! There are five basic aggravating types of persons with whom Jesus dealt:

1. Bigoted Traditionalists. This group of persons discussed secondary matters for years but never answered the truly ultimate questions.

2. Individualistic Traditionalists. These people lacked compassion and insisted that religion was "a private matter" without any social implications.

3. Hypocrites. These individuals stressed the outward form of religion. They pretended to be righteous, but inwardly they were "... full of dead *men's* bones, ..."

4. Commercialists. This group of persons wanted to turn religion into a profit-making venture and the House of God into a den of thieves.

5. Religious Actors. This group of persons wore long robes, made lengthy and loud prayers in public places, but lacked inwardness.

In short, Jesus must also have felt a sense of righteous anger and aggravation in facing these persons—but this was not his final word. "Judge not, that ye be not judged ..." He said. Judging others is a complicated venture. We nearly always condemn in others something which is wrong in ourselves. Again, if we are unhappy we derive a certain pleasure and measure of relief in criticizing others.

There have been—and are now—aggravating people who call themselves Christians—but that is not the final word of Jesus. The issue is how we deal with such persons. It is easy to criticize, but it is difficult to look for the positive in each individual. It is possible to correct a friend without attacking him or her at the same time. In the name of love, some people are afraid to be direct, but Jesus was direct and openly honest. But His rebukes were issued in the name of love. Loving criticism is difficult, but in the name of Jesus it is necessary.

HOW CAN WE GET FAITH?

> ... Believe on the Lord Jesus Christ, and thou shalt be saved, ...
> (Acts 16:31)

Paul and Silas had been thrown into prison. The jailer had dealt with them in his own way, which was harsh and cruel. Even after these insults, the two Disciples had not rebuked him, but rather they lifted up their voices to praise God. The jailer had never witnessed such faith and had asked the two Disciples what must be done to be saved. How can I get faith? This was his question.

We must clearly understand what is meant by faith. Some would say it is all a matter of temperament. Some persons are just naturally predisposed to believe. Others might reply that faith is a matter of killing the intellect, believing what you know isn't so just to gain a sense of security. But faith actually means a trust and confidence. Gradually the person or power in which I place trust molds personality.

How can we get faith? First of all, it must be understood that faith is not earned; even as we search for God, He is searching for us. There are four steps that unfold as faith is given. First, we begin to draw near the source of our trust; we enter into communion. Second, we surrender our pride and ask nothing. Third, we trust the source of our faith. And fourth, we maintain our communion over time with trust and service.

CAN FEAR BE CONQUERED?

... Be of good cheer: it is I; be not afraid.
(Mark 6:50)

In one of the teachings of Jesus, He describes certain times when our hearts grow weary out of fear. This issue is especially relevant during times of great need. We are afraid not only of the present moment but of the future.

Jesus challenged fear and offered courage. In Mark the sublime example of this attitude is found in the scene from the sea. As the winds blew against Jesus and His Disciples, they were afraid of drowning. "... be not afraid." Again and again in His ministry, Jesus told His Disciples not to be afraid.

We are never alone. Therein is the reason why His Disciples should not be afraid. Fear can be conquered by companionship with Jesus. He comes across the storms of life saying to us today: "... be not afraid."

CHAPTER

VII

EVERLASTING WORDS OF THE EVERLIVING LORD

THE EVER-PRESENT CHRIST

> ... lo, I am with you alway, *even* unto the end of the world.
> (Matthew 28:20)

In the four Gospels and in the Book of Acts, there are records of the words of Jesus to His Disciples after His resurrection. The final and last words of any person are important; how much more should we hear the words of our Lord who conquered death?

The words of the Gospel of Matthew, "... lo, I am with you alway, *even* unto the end of the world," can be considered along three lines: the place, the person, and the proclamation.

The Place. Matthew tells us that the place was a mountain where Jesus had appointed them. Eleven of the Disciples had assembled there, and it may be that up to 500 other believers were in attendance. It may be that this was the same mountain where earlier in His ministry Jesus had delivered the Sermon on the Mount.

It was a dramatic and climactic moment for all who had gathered. The Disciples were seeing the Risen Lord, in all His power, before He ascended into Heaven. They were going out into the world as His witnesses. His words were prefaced by a great affirmation: "... All power is given unto me in heaven and in earth." His words to the Disciples were meant to inspire their souls and give them courage for the work ahead.

The Person. The value of words is always strengthened by the character of the person who utters them. Who is this person speaking to the Disciples? First, it is the Risen Lord—the conqueror of death—who speaks. Second, the words are those of the Redeemer—the one who has been crucified for the sake of humanity. Third, it is the man Jesus—the one who has taken upon Himself human nature.

Jesus says, "I am ..." Who is He? According to the Gospel of John, this person may be called any of the following: the Bread of Life; the Good Shepherd; the Resurrection and the Life; the Way, Truth, and Life; Before Abraham. "... I am with you ..." This is the word of complete assurance—looking back, looking around, and looking ahead.

51

The Proclamation.   G. Campbell Morgan once said that a proclamation is more than a promise; it is a fact. Jesus did not promise the Disciples that He would be in their midst; He proclaimed His presence. He would always be with them.

His proclamation is one of perfect patience and power. He proclaims He will be with them, and us, in places of peril and difficulty. He proclaimed His presence in times of danger, during times of loneliness, and during times of temptation and testing.

"... lo, I am with you alway." He is here now. Whatever we do in His name and in His spirit, He is with us. Herein rests the ultimate source of authority and power of the Risen Lord. Herein is the Good News!

HIS WORLD MISSION

> ... All power is given unto me in heaven and in earth. Go ye therefore, and teach all nations, baptizing them in the name of the Father, and of the Son, and of the Holy Ghost: Teaching them to observe all things whatsoever I have commanded you: ...
>
> (Matthew 28:18-20)

It is an impressive fact that all four Gospels record the words of the Great Commission in one form or another. In fact, the differences in the Gospel records give us a fourfold emphasis of the one mission given by Jesus.

In the Gospels of Mark, Luke, and John the Great Commission, or plans for the world mission, was spoken eight days after His resurrection. In Matthew the words are recorded as being spoken almost immediately before His ascension and possibly to the eleven Disciples and 500 other people.

Let us notice the facts of Matthew's account:

1. The eleven Disciples went into Galilee, to a mountain where Jesus had appointed them. Jesus then came to the Disciples and perhaps to the 500 others, who would have been seeing Him for the first time since His resurrection.

2. As they looked on Him, they worshipped. The word worship here means absolute prostration in the presence of supremacy.

3. "... some doubted." This brief statement points to the validity of what took place; were the story a fabrication, it is not likely the authors would have wanted these words used. The word doubt as used in this passage indicates wavering, wondering, and perplexity. The people that had gathered could hardly believe what they were seeing; it was beyond their normal experiences.

What Jesus said at this moment is of lasting importance to all His Disciples. First was an affirmation of His authority. Second was a declaration of His mission.

Standing on the Resurrection side of His grave, Jesus affirmed simply all kingly authority on Heaven and earth. The word authority here does not mean the power of politics—that is, the right to utter the final verdict and pass sentence. Understood by the persons who heard Jesus, His affirmation meant a vindication of His ideals, a ratification of His purposes, and an initiation of a new age.

Jesus then proclaimed that the mission of His Disciples was to go to all nations; He broadened His appeal beyond the Jewish people. This declaration set the tone for the mission of His church: to be Disciples of Jesus, to bring the Good News to all people, and to teach all people about the Kingdom.

THE GOSPEL TO THE WHOLE CREATION

... Go ye into all the world, and preach the gospel to every creature.

(Mark 16:15)

The Resurrection events chronicled by Mark took place on the first day in the resurrected life of Jesus. The record in Matthew includes events that took place during the close of His 40 days and just prior to His ascension.

The day after His resurrection, as recorded by Mark, was one full of surprises. The cross had been a shattering blow to the Disciples; they had scattered and fled. With the dawn of the first day of the week, there had come to a little company of weeping women the consciousness that Jesus was not dead. A little later He had appeared to Mary. Later Peter and John had come to the place where His body had been lain and been convinced of His resurrection by the way in which His grave-clothes still lay undisturbed. At some hour in the first day, Jesus had joined two Disciples on their way to Emmaus and had made Himself known to them. These two, immediately after He had passed out of sight, had hurried back to Jerusalem to tell His Disciples what had happened. As they were speaking, Jesus stood materially manifest in their midst. It was on this precise occasion that Jesus spoke about the Gospel for all creation.

Jesus spoke about taking the Gospel to all creation, but we must carefully consider what He meant by Gospel. To do so, it is necessary to examine the story in Mark to discover the sequence of events.

1. Jesus appeared to Mary of Magdala. She carried the news to the mourning Disciples that she had actually seen Jesus alive. They did not believe her.

2. Jesus appeared in another form to two Disciples on the road to Emmaus. They also returned to the Disciples with their story, and they still did not believe.

3. Finally, Jesus stood in the Upper Room and His first words rebuked their disbelief; and then He immediately said: "... Go ye into all the world, and preach the gospel ..."

What is this Gospel? The Good News is that the Lord is risen! If we have only the cross, we have no good news. But the resurrection of Jesus is the demonstration of His victory over all opposing forces in the universe.

Jesus then uttered the following words: "He that believeth and is baptized shall be saved; but he that believeth not shall be damned. And these signs shall follow them that believe; In my name shall they cast out devils; they shall speak with new tongues; They shall take up serpents; and if they drink any deadly thing, it shall not hurt them; they shall lay hands on the sick, and they shall recover." It is important to observe that Jesus did not say these signs would accompany the preachers; the idea is *not* that those who proclaim the Resurrection shall work these signs as proof of His resurrection. It is that all persons who believe in Him would be brought into possession of the powers of God and may operate in the ways suggested, just as persons today may show different indications of God's supremacy over the world.

The Gospel is the living Lord. His resurrection means He has mastered death and overcome all the forces of evil that thwart God's purpose for His creation. These forces of evil include the confusion of tongues; material dislocations such as poisons or serpents; and illnesses, both physical and mental. In the power of the resurrected Lord, there is mastery over all such evil and healing from its curse.

The source of this power is indicated in the words of Jesus: "He that believeth and is baptized shall be saved; ..." The dynamic phrase is "... and is baptized ..." Essential baptism is in the Spirit of God. A person is anointed with new life, the old is washed away, and a new creature is full of the living Christ. Through this new creation, persons are then given restorative power over evil, social disorder, and all other destructive forces.

The followers of Jesus now go out into creation and into close relation with the wounded world, sharing its agony, in order to release the power of the Risen Lord.

PERFECT LOVE CASTETH OUT FEAR

> ... All hail.
>
>> (Matthew 28:9)
>
> ... Be not afraid: go tell my brethren that they go into Galilee, and there shall they see me.
>
>> (Matthew 28:10)

... Woman, why weepest thou? whom seekest thou? ...
(John 20:15)

... Mary. ... Touch me not; for I am not yet ascended to my
Father: but go to my brethren, and say unto them, I ascend un-
to my Father, and your Father; and to my God, and your God.
(John 20:16-17)

There are the words of Jesus spoken to women. All four Gospels record
the fact that women were the first to see the empty tomb and first to see
the Risen Lord. Two of the Gospels, Matthew and John, record the words
of Jesus to women.

Throughout His public ministry, Jesus spoke words of encouragement
to women. He was kind to women who brought their children to Him. He
valued the friendship of Mary and Martha in Bethany. He ministered to
women in need without regard to their race or status. His own mother
and other women stood beside Him at the cross. The status of women before Jesus should not be forgotten. While the Pharisees might thank God
they had not been born a gentile or woman, Jesus lifted women to equal
status with men. God does not know the arbitrary sexual barriers we
place between His children.

After His resurrection, Jesus appeared to a number of women. Among
them were: Mary of Magdala; Mary of Cleophas, mother of James, Joses,
and Salome; and Joanna, wife of a steward in Caesar's household. To all
those today who claim that women cannot occupy an equal place in the
church because the Disciples were men, it should be pointed out that the
first persons to encounter the Risen Lord were women; women were by
His side at the cross, and women carried the Good News to men who hid
away in the face of apparent defeat.

In Matthew's account, two women came early to the tomb to see the
sepulcher. They came out of love and loyalty. Suddenly, an angel appeared at the open grave, announcing: "He is not here: for he is risen, ..."
And as these women departed quickly from the tomb to bring word to
others, He met them. His first words to them were "... All hail." His second words were "... Be not afraid: ..."

In John's Gospel, Mary Magdalene had come early to the tomb and
stood before it weeping. She thought someone had stolen the body.
Then, Jesus appeared before her, though she did not know who He was,
saying: "... Woman, why weepest thou? whom seekest thou? ..." He then
called her by name, "... Mary." And then He charged her to tell the others
about His resurrection.

What do these words of Jesus to women mean?

In His first words, "... All hail." there is the heart of all that Jesus proposes for women. Be glad and be of good cheer: You are part of God's
plan, no matter what the culture dictates as your role. In the second

words, "Be not afraid: ..." there is hope for women. Fear not what others think; salvation is open to everyone and death has been conquered. In the third words, "... go tell ... ," there is the charge for women to participate fully in His mission. And in the fourth words, "... Why weepest thou? ... ," there is comfort, strength, and the promise of His presence.

PEACE BE UNTO YOU

> Then the same day at evening, being the first *day* of the week, when the doors were shut where the disciples were assembled for fear of the Jews, came Jesus and stood in the midst, and saith unto them, Peace *be* unto you.
>
> (John 20:19)

These words from John's Gospel are an inspiring record of the Risen Lord. John does not argue for readers to believe the Resurrection; he simply describes what happened.

"... Peace *be* unto you." Jesus spoke these words three times after His resurrection: to the Disciples behind closed doors, to these same Disciples as He commissioned them, and to the skeptical and fearful Thomas because of his unbelief. These words were not simply an ordinary salutation. The derivations of the word "peace" in Hebrew and Greek help us to see the deeper meaning. In Hebrew, the word is *shalom*, which has as its root meaning "adjusted for action." *Eirene* is the Greek word, actually meaning "to be joined together." Combined, the meaning of the words of Jesus relate to harmony, integration, and readiness for action.

What is the nature of this peace? First, it has individual implications. There is to be no inward division, but rather balance and harmony. There are social implications as well. There is to be no pride or prejudice, but rather acceptance of others. In relation to God, the word implies communion rather than rebellion and estrangement.

The amazing meaning of the word "peace" from the lips of the Risen Lord is that it symbolizes His benediction and promise to all those who follow after Him. This benediction is given to those who live in fear and anxiety, to those who are commissioned to be His Disciples, and to all the skeptical and fearful. St. Paul caught the meaning of this when he wrote to the Roman Christians: "Being therefore justified by faith, we have peace with God through our Lord Jesus Christ."

THE ASCENSION WORDS

> ... It is not for you to know the times or the seasons, which the Father hath put in his own power. But ye shall receive power, after that the Holy Ghost is come upon you: and ye shall be

witnesses unto me both in Jerusalem, and in all Judaea, and in Samaria, and unto the uttermost part of the earth.

(Acts 1:7-8)

The resurrection of Jesus was the central fact of the early faith of the Christian church. If one believes this, it is not difficult to believe in the ascension of the Christ, who passed into the unseen and immediate presence of God. All four Gospels refer directly or indirectly to the fact of His ascension, but the actual words are recorded in the Book of Acts.

Mark states, with his accustomed brevity, that after Jesus had spoken with them, He "... was received up into heaven, and sat on the right hand of God." Luke states that Jesus was "... carried up into heaven." Matthew concludes his Gospel with no direct reference to the Ascension, but clearly infers it. John does not refer to this event in his Gospel, but the Book of Revelation ushers in the presence of an ascended Lord. Paul repeatedly refers to the Ascension in his letter to the Romans. Peter, in his First Epistle, says that Jesus "... is gone into heaven, ..."

It is important, therefore, to consider the words of Jesus at the great hour of His ascension. To do this, we need to follow four lines of meditation: the occasion, the Disciples, the final words, and the value of His ascension.

The Occasion.   Forty days after His resurrection is the period of time the Risen Lord spent with His Disciples. After this period, at Bethany on the slopes of the Mount of Olives, He led them and was taken up into Heaven. As He was taken up, a cloud hid Him from their sight, and immediately two men spoke: "... Ye men of Galilee, why stand ye gazing up into heaven? this same Jesus, which is taken up from you into heaven, shall so come in like manner as ye have seen Him go into heaven." This was an hour full of glory and mystery.

The Disciples.   These were the men who had known Jesus for three years; they had seen Him crucified and then risen. Even after these experiences, these same men could ask: "... wilt thou at this time restore again the kingdom to Israel?" They still could not comprehend fully what He had done. After His departure, however, they returned to Jerusalem with great joy.

The Final Words.   There was a threefold message from Jesus. First, He issued a warning: "... It is not for you to know the times or the seasons, which the Father hath put in his own power." Second, He issued a promise: "But ye shall receive power, after that the Holy Ghost is come upon you: ..." And third, he offered His commission: "... ye shall be witnesses unto me ..."

The Values of His Ascension.   Jesus now assumes universal power; He is no longer a teacher or prophet but the Lord. Through the cross and Resurrection, Jesus attains His glory. Through His sacrifice, humanity is provided the model for living and given its mission on earth.

VIII
CHRIST: THE ANSWER TO THE WORLD'S NEEDS

... God so loved the world. ...
(John 3:16)
... I am the light of the world: ...
(John 8:12)
The field is the world; ...
(Matthew 13:38)
... Go ye into all the world, ...
(Mark 16:15)

These four sayings of Jesus center around the theme of the world. The first saying is the great truth concerning the heart of God, His love, and His purpose for the world. The second saying is the great claim of Christ concerning His purpose. The third statement is Christ's teaching for His Disciples concerning their responsibility. The fourth saying is the great commission to proclaim the Gospel to the whole world.

The church must keep this world view in mind as it goes about its mission. Our understanding of the world must be seen in the light of the Gospel, the Kingdom, and the imperatives of Jesus.

THE WORLD

The world is one in the mind of Jesus and one in the heart and purpose of God. Defining the task of His followers, Jesus said: "The field is the world: ..."

The world is unified, in spite of man-made differences. As the poet Wordsworth said, "We all of us have a human heart." During this century, the world has become a giant village rather than distinct nation-states. Rapid communications, the independence of commerce and industry, cooperative services, and international relations have all joined to bring us closer together.

Lovers of art have commented on the marked difference between the works of Watts and those of Turner. Watts looks at things and portrays them close at hand; Turner looks at things and depicts them in the distance. For the greater part of our lives, we see life in the range of vision suggested by Watts. The world is close about us; its duties and cares absorb us. We are immersed in detail. It is salubrious to break the chain of our captivity and to win detachment so that we may get a whole sense of reality—a distant picture.

When the monk of the Grande Chartreuse was asked why the windows of the monastery faced inwards on the courtyard instead of outwards upon the hills, he replied that he and his fellows had not come there to look at mountains. It is very easy for each of us to let all the windows of our lives turn in upon our own affairs. We must, however, find the birth of a new outlook so that we may open windows in blind walls and see the green landscape.

Nothing is more impressive in the New Testament than to see how Jesus expanded the horizons of the early believers. From a small movement, His person and message included the entire universe. His mission could not be contained by one geographical location but burst into the world itself.

How can we become world conscious? We can: first, make the church more than a Western reality and broaden our message to reach those who do not speak our language or follow our customs; and second, remember that in Christ there is neither Jew nor Gentile, that Jesus came to save the world, and that in setting up barriers between persons we are violating His Gospel. Surely now at this hour, Christians may unite under one Lord, who came as a servant to all people for all time.

THE WORLD'S ONE GOSPEL

> ... Go ye into all the world, and preach the Gospel to every creature.
>
> (Mark 16:15)

The Gospel offers the claim that it is the truth about God and humanity, about the purpose of history, and the end to which that purpose is bringing the world. The lack of understanding of this Good News is evident in modern Christianity so that often the message goes no further than our neighborhood. But the Gospel is the world.

The incurably religious nature of mankind is a great asset when we approach the consideration of the Gospel that claims to be appropriate and adequate to all the needs of the world. All faiths have some common elements. The object of reverence and awe is a supreme being. The subject of faith and service is the human spirit, mind, and soul. The forms of worship are prayer and sacrifice.

The conditions to be met for a world gospel are its universality, adequacy, and absoluteness.

Universality.   The Gospel must submit to the test of human experience on every field and under varieties of circumstance. It must prove itself equal to all the demands of life; in short, it must be universal.

Whereas the gods of many non-Christians are local deities—gods of the nation or tribe—the God of Jesus has unrestricted providence. He is no respecter of nations. Jesus Himself lived in a time of pronounced national feeling. There was a religious, social, and racial barrier of the most exclusive kind. Jesus transcended all such distinctions based on race or nationality. He welcomed to His friendship Greeks, Romans, Samaritans, and Jews.

Human experience presents a variety of form and type: Jesus provides a response to each. He presents Himself in the light of individual and cultural differences but is still the same Lord. The Gospel admits no differences or restrictions for entrance into the presence of Jesus. This is a truth we would do well to remember in our churches. If we dare to reject a person because of race or income, we are violating the commandments of Jesus and are no longer fit to be called His Disciples.

Adequacy.   This one world Gospel must be adequate. None should be able to say: "I tried it, and it failed." It must be equal to the strain of experience, sufficient for the demands of life, and strong enough to meet all the dangers of life.

The Disciples were subjected to a crucial test by the trust of a man who brought his afflicted son to them to be cured. They could not help, and the father reported the failure to Jesus. "... bring him hither to me." He said. This is typical of His adequacy. Of the problems that remain unresolved and the difficulties unsurmounted—"... bring them hither to me."

It is true that there are abuses today, even in His name. We have not always made Christendom Christian. But these exist in spite of the Gospel; the Good News is adequate, if not through the graces of the church then through the personality of its founder.

Absoluteness.   The Gospel for the world must be absolute. It cannot be temporary and relative nor lost in the past or tied to the present. Although Jesus lived during a period of history, His Gospel did not die when that era died. Every new generation gives some new insight into the truth.

But what is the content of this Gospel, having met the tests of adequacy, universality, and absoluteness?

First, the Gospel speaks with authority about God. In some world religions, God is passive while humanity is seeking. In the Gospel, God is actively seeking; mankind obeys if it will. There is no teaching about God that can compare with that of Jesus. He has a clear and intimate consciousness of God; there is no fear or distance. Where He could not speak the truth, He acted it, lived it, and loved it. The cross was the final act of faith in God; it was the expression of divine love bearing the terrible abuse of humanity.

Second, the Gospel speaks with authority about humanity. Because Jesus was a man, He made important the human nature—even the single individual. Jesus redeemed humanity; out of the wasteland of human life, He takes a person and makes him or her whole. Redeemed beauty is as great as unfallen glory.

Third, the Gospel speaks of sin. There is an instinctive, incontrovertible sense of wrong in creation. The Gospel faces this fact squarely, tears the mask away, and describes sin for what it is· a blow at the heart of God. But sin is also judged at the cross—and forgiven.

Fourth, the Gospel speaks about the conquest of death and about life after death. "... Who shall go over the sea for us, ..." asks an ancient voice. The sure answer is: Jesus has gone over the sea. Neither life nor death shall separate us from Him. We have the profound assurance of His presence, even unto death and beyond.

THE KINGDOM TO COME

The Kingdom of God is central to the teaching and ministry of Jesus. Many of His parables highlight the Kingdom. John the Baptist cried in the wilderness, "... the kingdom of God is at hand: ..." When Jesus began His public ministry, His words were: "... The time is fulfilled, and the kingdom of God is at hand: ..."

For many centuries the hopes of Israel had been sustained by the vision of the Messiah's Kingdom. Prophet and psalmist saw afar this golden age. God would establish His Kingdom in the history and experience of His people.

Jesus made it clear early in His ministry that the Kingdom of God was not to come by way of political organization, military revolution, or public demonstration. It was to come by the slow processes of growth and unobtrusive development. One day Jesus called two men to follow Him, then four, and these became twelve. At the close of His earthly ministry there were 120 assembled in the Upper Room. On the day of Pentecost there were 3,000. And finally we are told that "... a great multitude, ... of all nations, and kindreds, and people, and tongues, stood before the throne, and before the Lamb ..." All this is not to say that the Kingdom is to be measured by the number of converts, but rather that it is a process at work in history.

The Kingdom derives its character from the King. Jesus is the first essential of the Kingdom. He is to inaugurate the reign of God in the hearts of humanity. He does not suit His words to fit the common conceptions of the Kingdom; the Kingdom of God is primary and more important than political conquests.

Plato said the first essential of an ideal state was that people should have right ideas about God, and he advised that these should be taught to children. Tolstoy said that the man who seeks his own advantage is bad, the man who seeks the good opinion of others is weak, the man who promotes the happiness of others is virtuous, but the man who seeks God is great. God first, the rest follows. "... seek ye the kingdom ..." Jesus said. The character of the Kingdom, therefore, is the reign of God in our souls, expressing itself in all areas of our existence.

The dream of a unified empire or world has inspired the imagination in all ages. Conquest had its opportunity with Alexander and Napoleon but fell short. Commerce has attempted to unify the world, but war has dashed all possibilities of doing so with economics. Culture has sought a worldly domain, but culture by itself cannot cut across decades of mistrust. Unfortunately, we have often built the notion of one world upon commerce, culture, or conquest. But the Kingdom of God is the basis for a philosophy of one world. World cohesion is dependent upon spiritual communion. Jesus breaks down all cultural, racial, and national barriers; in His fellowship, every dividing passion and prejudice must die.

The faithful of all generations, moreover, are in the membership of the Kingdom. "... ye shall see Abraham, and Isaac, and Jacob, and all the prophets, in the kingdom of God, ..." The Kingdom transcends our own history and, yet, is part of it. All ages bring their gifts to the Kingdom; they are united in the sainthood of believers. Without the gifts of the past, we are not complete; without us, they have no voice in the present.

The Kingdom is a universal reality; Jesus swept the whole world in the field of His vision. An extraordinary variety of peoples were represented in the multitude that assembled in Jerusalem on the Day of Pentecost. Paul corresponded with people in widely scattered districts. John's vision on Patmos saw a multitude of nations and people forming one company. The Gospel, therefore, announced a Kingdom that is not the province of one culture or one people, but a universal proclamation. The Temple of Peace at the Hague is impressive with its universal symbolism. The entrance gates are from Germany and the terraced steps from Scandanavian countries. The clock in the tower is from Switzerland; the tapestries are from Japan; the carpets are from Turkey; the pictures are from France; and the stained glass windows are from Britain. A statue in the spacious stairway represents Christ of the Andes from Argentina. All the best of nations are gathered together in one place. But the chief cornerstone is Jesus. There is unity in diversity, just as many colors in the rainbow blend into reconciling art.

THE ONE IMPERATIVE

Run ye to and fro through the streets of Jerusalem and see ... if ye can find a man, ...
(Jeremiah 5:1)

... I sought for a man among them, that should make up the hedge, and stand in the gap before me for the land: ... but I found none.
(Ezekiel 22:30)

How can I, except some man should guide me?
(Acts 8:31)

... a man shall be as an hiding place from the wind, and a covert from the tempest; as rivers of water in a dry place, as the shadow of a great rock in a weary land.
(Isaiah 32:2)

These four texts set before our minds a single thought. God, the Gospel, and the condition of the world require the human dimension if the Kingdom is to come. "I dressed the wounds, God healed him," is the inscription over the gateway of the French College of Surgeons. This suggests the inevitable union of two forces, God and humanity, working together.

There are, it is true, many activities in which God is independent of human action. By His own might, He made the heavens and earth; He formed the earth from His own power. These are parts of the creative process that do not require human intervention. But there are activities in which human beings are indispensable. God has stored all the earth with productive qualities, but man must furrow the ground and sow the seed. The quarries are packed with stone, but man must chisel and form the stones into homes. God will not do for human beings what they can do for themselves.

The greatest deposit God has placed in the world is the Gospel. For its growth, God asks for human obedience and love. The Gospel is adequate for the world, but the world needs to act.

The one imperative of the Gospel is that human beings must decide in favor of the Gospel. The Good News requires us to dedicate our lives anew and utterly to Him, who loved us first and gave His life for many.

IX

CHRIST AND THE WOMEN IN THE NEW TESTAMENT

The status of women before Jesus has often been forgotten, as if Christianity were the province of men alone. It is true that in many world religions the man is central. Remember that the Pharisees thanked God that they were Gentiles, not women! Some ancient holy men even walked with their eyes to the ground, for fear of seeing a woman! But Jesus lifted women to their rightful place in God's creation, for sexual distinctions before God are a human invention—God created both male and female in His image.

Jesus ministered to a number of women during His time on earth. Fourteen names of women appear in the New Testament. These include: Mary of Magdala; Mary, His mother; Mary of Bethany; Martha of Bethany; Salome, mother of James and John; Joanna, the wife of Herod's steward; Mary of Cleophas; the Samaritan woman at the well; the woman who clutched His garment; the Syrophoenician woman; the condemned woman; the widow at the treasury; the weeping daughters of Jerusalem; and Pilate's wife.

In each of His encounters with the women mentioned above there is a diverse response, just as the women themselves are distinct personalities. But there is a response nonetheless—for women are given status and meaning in His ministry.

MARY OF MAGDALA

Mary of Magdala was the first person who met with and talked to the Risen Christ. The word Magdala means the city in which she lived. This Mary has often been confused with the woman in Simon's house or as the sinner called Magdalene.

What do we know about Mary of Magdala?

First, she was a woman possessed of seven demons (Luke 8:2). Here, we should be careful to note that this might have meant that she had a physical disability or emotional disorder; we do not know which of these is accurate. She was a woman of means, but more importantly a woman who showed deep dedication and devotion to Jesus, both at the cross and at His tomb. She was there, when others had fled.

What was Christ's method with her? First, He freed her from the mastery of evil spirits. He cast them out. Second, He called her to a new life, to be a witness to His Gospel. One recalls here the great account of their meeting on the Resurrection morning. He called her by name, "Mary." He issued a command to her: "... Touch me not; ..." And He gave her the Good News: "... go to my brethren, and say unto them, I ascend unto my Father, and your Father; and to my God, and your God."

Jesus helped Mary to attain her place among God's children by delivering her from sin. He took away the "demons" of lust and passion. More than this, He commissioned her to be His servant, a witness to the power of the Risen Lord. For those who want to lower the status of women in the church, let them read the account of Mary, who brought the Good News to men!

MARY, THE MOTHER OF JESUS

Protestants often do not comment upon Mary, the mother of Jesus, thinking this to be a thought for the Catholic Church alone. While there is no scriptural basis for making Mary divine, neither is there a scriptural basis for neglecting her. There is every reason to understand Mary, for she is the symbol of womanly power.

The relationship of Jesus to His mother consecrates the role of women as mothers, those who nurture the human infant from the earliest moments of life. Mary can be seen in two major roles: as a mother and as a Disciple.

As a mother, Mary was certain of the conviction of God upon her Son. She understood His mission. She also agreed to this role, as is evidenced by His consecration at the age of 12. She also showed concern for her Son; on His death, she came to take Him away. And finally, she showed constancy to the end, since she stood by the cross.

As a Disciple, Mary was confident of His power, as evidenced by the episode of the marriage feast at Cana. She also showed a capacity to learn from Him. Moreover, she cultivated the humble spirit, continuing steadfast in prayer.

How did Jesus react to His mother? He certainly told her about His mission, as evidenced by the scene in the Temple when He was 12 and He explained to her that He was about to do His Father's work. At Capernaum, He told her that His family was more than kin. Finally, at the cross, He cared for her, even at His last moments, by commending her to the loving care of one of His Disciples.

In Christ's relationship to His mother, we can see that this intimate child/mother interchange is important to God. More importantly, however, we see that Jesus went beyond family ties, expressing the thought that the Kingdom of God was not to be rooted in kinship.

MARY OF CLEOPHAS

It is probable that the Mary of Cleophas (John 19:25) and Mary, the mother of James and Joses (Matthew 27:56), are the same person. This person represents the theme of feminine ministry in sorrow, because her name is found wholly during the passion days of Jesus.

Mary of Cleophas was one of the women who stood by Jesus at the cross (John 19:25). She also went with Mary Magdalene to the tomb where He was buried. Finally, she was told by the Risen Lord to tell His Disciples about His resurrection. She was a Disciple who carried the Good News to the Apostles.

We are not told that Jesus spoke a single word to this Mary during His long hours of suffering. Perhaps earlier in Galilee He had talked with her, but this is not recorded. Yet, it was this woman who stood by Him at the cross and met Him as the Risen One. From the agony of His death, she learned the meaning of suffering; in His resurrection she understood the redemptive power of love that is able to cast out fear. She is symbolic of the ministry of compassion and devotion.

MARY AND MARTHA OF BETHANY

Mary and Martha of Bethany were sisters, although the Gospel pictures of them show two personalities. There are three references in the Gospels about these two women. First, in Luke 10:38-42, there is a record of the visit of Jesus to the home of His friends in Bethany. This was a day of prosperity and gladness. In the midst of His public ministry, Jesus went to a home, where He was accustomed to finding hospitality and sanctuary, with these two sisters. In John 11:1-46, we find the account of a day of gloom. Lazarus, their brother, has taken seriously ill and dies. Jesus is seen again, coming to this home and ministering to each of them. And, of course, He raises Lazarus from the dead. Finally in John 12:1-9, we find the record of a day of mystery. The time of this event is six days before the Passover. The sisters make Him supper, and Martha serves it. It was on this occasion that Mary brought a pound of ointment and anointed Him. Here, then, are three pictures of the sisters in times of despair and great hope.

Jesus dealt with these two women as individuals, and it is important to note this fact.

In the first picture we have of the dealing with Martha, it is with her as a loving hostess who is determined to do everything in her power to make the visit of Jesus bright and hopeful. In the midst of all her work to make the visit pleasant, she notices that Mary is not busy and complains of this to Jesus. He talks to her, telling her that she was so busy and distracted that she failed to notice the "one thing" important to life. She needed concentration, or the will to do one thing, in order to find peace. A second picture of Martha is during a time of calamity; she protests to Jesus that Lazarus might not have died had He been there. He responded to her: "... I am the resurrection, and the life: ..." A third portrait we have of Martha is found in a wonderful description: "... Martha served: ..." She had found her Lord in a new way; she still was doing "many things" but now had power in knowing the "one thing" necessary for true life.

In His dealings with Mary, we often get the picture of Mary as sentimental and one who would sit quietly at His feet. Here is an activity of devotion and of inner resources. In a second portrait, we find Mary sitting alone, quietly going about the work in the home. It is the occasion of the death of Lazarus, and Jesus wept. At His feet, Mary learned about the compassion of God. Finally, in the third scene, Mary is again at His feet. But, out of devotion and love, she provides ointment for His body. Jesus does not rebuke her.

What is the message from our understanding of His dealings with these two sisters? First, Jesus calls women into His spiritual fellowship. Second, He welcomes all who give Him hospitality or who, in His spirit, give comfort to the homeless and needy. And third, Jesus calls all to make time for God. At His feet all of us may find the strength and courage to face life if we would put first things first.

PILATE'S WIFE

The character of Pilate's wife appears only for a moment in the New Testament and that in the Gospel of Matthew. Yet in this one account, there is an inspired message.

In order to understand Pilate's wife, we must first understand Pilate. Pontius Pilate represented Tiberius, the Roman emperor, as procurator of Judea and Samaria. He was the sixth procurator and during his meeting with Jesus had been in power 11 years. Twice before he had nearly plunged the city into insurrection by introducing images of deities. Once, he had offended the Jews by carrying into the city his imperial standard which bore the image of the emperor. On another occasion he appropriated from the temple treasury the "corban," or revenue from redemption vows, in order to build an aqueduct. He suppressed riots by sending his soldiers among the people and arming them with concealed daggers.

Tradition has said that Pilate's wife's name was Claudia Procla; she was Roman by birth, abandoning her original faith to accept Jehovah. As early as the Church Father Origen, she is said to have become a Christian. During the time when Pilate was to make a decision about Jesus, she sent her husband a message: "... Have thou nothing to do with that just man: for I have suffered many things this day in a dream because of him." She called Jesus righteous and urged Pilate to have nothing to do with Him. Surely she must have felt trapped between her concern for her husband and the warnings of a dream. But she told her husband to let Jesus go—for this single moment there was an act of justice in the evil of the empire. She became the witness for this righteous man in the political arena, while most others were calling for His crucifixion.

THE WEEPING WOMEN OF JERUSALEM

Only in Luke's Gospel do we have the record of the weeping women, and this account is brief. The occasion of the event is along the Via Dolo rosa, or Sorrowful Way, on the way from the Praetorium up to the green hill outside the city of Jerusalem. The night of trials was over; Jesus had been scourged, the crown of thorns placed upon His head, and He had been sentenced to death. He was led forth, carrying His own cross.

But He had stumbled under the heavy weight of the cross. One Simon of Cyrene had been ordered by the Roman soldiers to carry His cross. There came, then, a great multitude of people, including women who lamented His fate. These were women who lived in Jerusalem and who could not withhold their tears in seeing His suffering.

Jesus responded to these weeping women: "... Daughters of Jerusalem, weep not for me, but weep for yourselves, and for your children. For, behold, the days are coming, in the which they shall say, Blessed are the barren, and the wombs that never bare, and the paps which never gave suck. Then shall they begin to say to the mountains, ... Cover us. For if they do these things in a green tree, what shall be done in the dry?" Here, in these words, was the prediction of doom that would fall upon Jerusalem. Here, too, are the words of infinite tenderness, as He saw the plight of these defenseless women. He told them not to weep for Him, but for themselves. He called upon them for tears of repentance as well.

In His words to these weeping women, there is the revelation of His vicarious suffering for others. He felt and suffered for their tribulation. He chose His own death, but His heart went out to the sufferings of others. There is surely something of the heart of God here, for God suffers when His children suffer. In the mystery of His suffering, evil is transformed and God is revealed as the companion who suffers with us when we hurt deeply and are in pain. If we could truly believe this, we could find the strength necessary, for God can wipe away our tears and even weep with us.

CHRIST AND THE WIDOW AT THE TREASURY

In the case of the widow at the treasury, deeds speak louder than words, for the woman in this story is not named and she did not even speak to Jesus. Neither do we have the words of Jesus to this woman but only His words to His Disciples about her. It would seem very likely that this widow did not know Jesus spoke about her. All these factors notwithstanding, Jesus understood this woman's solitary gift and raised her sacrifice to holiness.

Both Mark and Luke record the event of the widow at the treasury. Mark contrasts the gift of the widow with that of the rich casting much money into the treasury; Luke does likewise. Very little is said about the widow except that she cast in "... two mites, ..." which is infinitely smaller than our dime. She was a daughter of Israel and a worshipper of the Living God. In spite of her poverty, she gave everything she could to God and all that she could afford.

In appraising this widow, Jesus told His Disciples that she had given more than the rich. She had given her gift freely and with devotion; it cost her something. Others had cast their gifts out of their surplus; she had made a sacrifice.

What can we learn from this woman? First, God watches over us, even those who seem lost in the crowd. He does not judge us by what is obvious but understands the spirit behind the external. Second, God judges the motives behind our gifts. If our gift is truly a sacrifice and is offered to God in devoted love, it matters not whether it be large or small.

THE WOMAN IN SIMON'S HOUSE

In the midst of the public ministry of Jesus, there came a time when the religious rulers were showing increased hostility toward His teachings. Some said He was too severe; others claimed He was overly joyful. It was during this time that a certain Pharisee, named Simon, invited Jesus to dinner at his house. It was in one of the Galilean towns, perhaps Nain, but most probably Capernaum. Simon had invited Jesus in order to observe Him at close quarters; it was not, therefore, an especially cordial invitation. We have to think of Simon because, in considering the woman of this episode, we see her in comparison with him. They belonged to the opposite strata of society. Simon was the suburban elite; the woman belonged to the slums. He was the educated leader; she was the outcast. Luke describes the woman as "... a woman in the city, which was a sinner, ..." This is obvious, since it appears her sin was one of sexual immorality. She came to dinner out of obvious devotion to Jesus, for it had cured her of her sin. She brought along with her an alabaster of ointment; standing behind His feet, she anointed them. As she did so, her emotion swept over her and tears began to fall.

Simon the Pharisee wanted to know if Jesus understood what kind of woman she was. Jesus responded with a question, a parable, and a deduction.

First, He asked "... Simon, Seest thou this woman?" What He really asked was: Have you really seen all there is to know about this woman? Have you seen her salvation? Second, He told Simon the Parable of the Two Debtors, about one owing ten times as much as the other. Whom would the lender forgive most? Third, Jesus pointed out that the woman was greatly in debt, had been pardoned and, therefore, greatly loved the One who had forgiven her. And He said to the woman, "... Thy sins are forgiven."

In this story we have the sure knowledge that Jesus has the power to forgive sins, no matter how great. He can make new creations out of us. And we have the knowledge that through this forgiveness our devotion is accepted.

THE CONDEMNED WOMAN

The weight of external and internal evidence suggests that John 8:1 through 8:11 did not form part of the Gospel as John wrote it, but was an interpretation written at a later time. Possibly these verses were added by Papias, who was bishop in the first half of the second century, and taken from oral history. There is, however, no reason to doubt the truth of the story, even if it was not written by John.

Jesus was in the midst of His teaching at the Temple in Jerusalem. It was during one of the great feasts of Israel. It was in the morning; as he was teaching, the scribes and Pharisees brought before Him a woman accused of adultery. We know nothing more about her, except that for all practical arguments she was viewed as a condemned criminal. Obviously, the Jewish leaders were slyly testing the reaction of Jesus to this woman.

The leaders asked Jesus whether the woman should be stoned. Instead of replying with words, Jesus stooped down and wrote on the ground; He turned His face away from them. And then He responded: "... He that is without sin among you, let him first cast a stone at her." The principle He stated was deceptively simple: Sinlessness is the condition of exacting a penalty. He did not discuss Roman or Jewish Law. The rulers left "... convicted by *their own* conscience, ..." Jesus and the woman were alone.

Jesus asked her two questions. "... Woman, where are those thine accusers?" And, "... hath no man condemned thee?" Her only response was: "... No man, Lord." He then absolved her, telling her to sin no more.

Jesus provides forgiveness to all those who have broken the laws of God. He absolves, but He also requires that we sin no more.

THE SYROPHOENICIAN WOMAN

The story of the Syrophoenician woman differs from other episodes already described in that this woman was not Jewish. As such, it shows the presence of Christ against racial prejudices.

Matthew (15:21-28) and Mark (7:24-30) both record this story, and both are careful to note the woman was a member of another race and religion.

Mark begins the story with an interesting statement: "... he could not be hid." We know from other accounts that Jesus could retreat from the crowds, but in this case He could not. Why not? I would say that He could not hide away from the need of this woman; in the presence of agony, He could not retreat.

Although not a member of the Jewish race or religion, what shined through about this woman was her love and her faith. She came to seek help for her daughter, who she thought was tortured by a demon. She came because she had heard about Jesus and His power.

Jesus responded: "... it is not meet to take the children's bread, and to cast it unto the dogs." He did not mean by this the image of wild dogs, but rather tame dogs. Her reply was instant and full of wit: "... Yes, Lord: yet the dogs under the table eat of the children's crumbs." For her saying, Jesus healed her daughter.

The abiding message of this story is that Jesus crosses all culturally imposed barriers of race and nation for those who are in need. He understands that faith cannot be contained in national or racial superiority myths but cuts across all man-made barriers.

THE WOMAN IN THE CROWD

Three of the Evangelists record the story of the ministry of Jesus to an unnamed woman in the crowd who touched the border of His garment and was healed of her disease.

Both Mark and Luke point out that the woman had seen many physicians but had not been cured. She was suffering from an issue of the blood. Leviticus 15:19-27 provides careful instructions for the treatment of this ailment. Persons with the disease were to be segregated from the company of the faithful as a hygienic measure. The belief was that the disease was the result of sin. For 12 years this woman had been shut off from normal social interaction.

We do not know if this woman had ever seen Jesus before, but she had certainly heard stories about His miracles. She said within herself, "... If I may touch but his clothes, I shall be whole." She came behind Him from the crowd and clutched the border of His garment. The Greek word used here definitely means clutched or grasped. And she was instantly cured. She started to slip away quietly without being noticed.

Jesus knew something different had taken place; He understood the difference between the jostle of a crowd and the clutch of faith.

The woman then came forth, falling down before Him to confess the truth. "... Daughter, ..." He said tenderly, "thy faith hath made thee whole; go in peace, ..."

If we understand correctly this story of His encounter with women, we find that any person who feels great need can grasp for His healing power and find peace. And, having made an open confession, those who clutch for His power can be healed.

THE WOMAN AT THE WELL IN SAMARIA

To the Jews, the Samaritans were foreigners with whom they had little dealing. In the story of the dealing of Jesus with the woman of Samaria, we again encounter the presence of a Person who did not know racial or national boundaries and who dismissed all the petty concerns that divide humanity into camps and kingdoms.

Jesus opened and closed the conversation with this woman. The woman was one who lived in sin, caught in the grip of passion. She was also a religious woman, talking about "... our father Jacob, ..." Jesus appealed to her kindness, curiosity, and deepest desires. He pointed out her sin and then announced Himself as the Messiah.

In spite of all degradation and failure, Jesus makes His appeal to the deepest realities of our spiritual nature. But He does not do so without having us face our sins directly. He probes our inner spirits, making us face the evil within. So much human wreckage is the result of false attempts to reach legitimate needs; Jesus sets out legitimate attempts to reach legitimate needs.

SALOME, THE MOTHER

There are three occasions in the New Testament when Salome is mentioned.

In Matthew 20:20-28, the mother of the sons of Zebedee came to Jesus asking Him: "... Grant that these my two sons may sit, the one on thy right hand, and the other on the left, in thy kingdom." Here we see a mother's ambition for her sons, although based on only partial information about the mission of Jesus. Mark, too, reports about Salome, noting that she was seen at the cross, standing by His suffering. In Mark 16:1, Salome comes to the tomb with Mary Magdalene and Mary, the mother of James, in order to anoint His body with spices. At the tomb, she is confronted by an angel announcing His resurrection. She was thus one of the first to hear of His resurrection and to be a witness.

Jesus also ministered to Salome in responding to her motherly questions. First, He declared that it was not His decision about who entered the Kingdom and that His role was to give His life as a ransom for many. Second, before the cross, Salome was shown that the meaning of His mission was redemptive love. Third, before the empty tomb, Salome must have known the verification of His mission: that love triumphs over death.

There is a lesson here about the ambition of parents for their children. In spite of the rather forward request of Salome, Jesus does not rebuke her. She was expressing a normal protective feeling for her sons; she wanted them to have some sense of security. But Jesus set another role for her children: that of being ministers unto others. This should be the great motive of parental love: that our children shall have the strength to be witnesses to the power of creative suffering and love for others.

JOANNA, WIFE OF HEROD'S SERVANT

There are only two references to Joanna in the Gospel records. Nonetheless, Joanna was part of a faithful company of women who followed Jesus.

In Luke 8:3, we read that with other women Joanna "... ministered unto him of their substance." In Luke 24:10, it is reported that Joanna and other women reported certain things to the Disciples.

Who was Joanna? Her husband was Herod's steward; he dispensed food, money, and household possessions. Her home was probably at Tiberius, the capital city of Herod. She probably had a physical infirmity, which had been healed by Jesus around the Sea of Galilee. After this experience, she had left the court of Herod and served Him. She also was one of the first witnesses to the Resurrection.

Jesus responded to her, first, by healing her of the physical infirmity. And He accepted her support and service, vindicating this in His resurrection. She gave her physical aid and substance; He gave of Himself to her and others through His life.

THE WOMEN AT PENTECOST

Throughout His ministry, women were on equal footing with men, sometimes in opposition to men themselves. Before and after His cross and resurrection, women received His blessing without any suggestion of inferiority or being secondary in importance to men. For those who think otherwise, perhaps another reading of the Gospel records is in order.

On the Day of Pentecost, however, the rightful place of women as Disciples is finally and clearly revealed: Women face God and life on the same terms as men, being given openly the Spirit of God Himself. As

Luke writes: "These all continued with one accord in prayer and supplication, with the women, and Mary, the mother of Jesus, and with his brethren." (Acts 1:14) Again, in Acts, we find all the Disciples together "... in one place."

At Pentecost, we find women facing God and receiving the Spirit of God naturally and without hesitation on an equal basis with men. There is no distinction at all between male and female and no arbitrary setting apart of a male priesthood and feminine class. As Peter quoted from the Prophet Joel during his sermon: "... I will pour out my spirit upon all flesh; and your sons and your daughters shall prophesy, ..." Later, Paul would write: "There is neither Jew nor Greek, there is neither bond nor free, there is neither male nor female: for ye are all in Christ Jesus."

After Pentecost, the New Testament is filled with the stories of women who served the early church. There were women who provided Christian homes (the mother of Mark, Eunice, and Lois), women who served as helpmates (Priscilla), and women who were organizers (Lydia and Dorcas).

Jesus did not set up the arbitrary distinctions of male and female for His Gospel. The gift was given freely, and it is ours if we would follow the Master. The Good News is one of liberation for male and female, rich and poor, and old and young.

THE GOSPEL ACCORDING TO CHRIST'S ENEMIES

sually Christians think they know about Jesus from His friends. From that hour at Caesarea Philippi when He first announced His cross and resurrection—and through to Easter Day—we consider the Gospel according to those who were His Disciples.

Yet there is another way to study the life and teachings of Jesus and that is to recall the words of those who opposed Him. The extent of their testimony is such that it comprises the entire Gospel in its essential facts. Indeed, if by some unthinkable catastrophe the Bible should become lost to us except for what His enemies said of Him, we should still have a record of the Eternal Spirit of God. Although His foes wanted to insult and slander Him, they spoke more truly than they realized—as most people do in His presence. In their hostility they witnessed to His power and the truth. It is to the glory of the Gospel that many have become His Disciples through the word of His enemies.

There are five sayings of His enemies that will be considered:
1. "... This man receiveth sinners, ..."
2. "... this man doeth many miracles."
3. "... Never man spake ..."
4. "... we know that thou art true, ..."
5. "He saved others; himself he cannot save."

THIS MAN RECEIVETH SINNERS

This saying is recorded in Luke 15:1-2. It took place on a Sabbath Day when Jesus had been an invited guest in the home of one of the Pharisees. The whole day is recorded for us by Luke in Chapter 14. We can recall the happenings as follows:
1. Jesus invited to dinner, along with a man with a withered hand.
2. Jesus criticized the fellow guests.
3. Jesus corrected the host.
4. Jesus told a story about excuses.
5. Jesus left the home, and great multitudes followed Him and He said:

"If any *man* come to me, and hate not ... his own life ... And whosoever doth not bear his cross, and come after me, cannot be my disciple."

All the publicans and sinners were drawing near to Jesus to hear what He might say. It was then that the Pharisees and scribes uttered this sentence about Him: "... This man receiveth sinners, and eateth with them."

It should be remembered that the religious rulers of that day passed through three stages in their attitudes toward Jesus. At first they patronized Him. Then they criticized Him. And finally they sought to kill Him. This comment upon His attitude toward sinners showed deep resentment and criticism of Jesus.

What the rulers really said to Jesus was not only that He received sinners, but also that He was contaminated by them. They simply could not explain away Jesus and, with a sneer, they tried to dismiss Him. It would be difficult for us to capture all the venom they might have used in their tone of voice.

What His critics failed to understand was that as Jesus dealt with sinners, so, too, did God. These sinning people were healed and made pure again. These sinning people were reborn. These sinning people were uplifted and changed. No wonder, then, the Gospel came as an offense to the pious and a release for the oppressed. Jesus communicated the redeeming power of God's love for all creation and most especially the outcasts.

We might well apply this criticism to our contemporary age. We may want to believe that Jesus came only to the pure, to the wealthy, and to those who are religiously prepared. But He came for those who were lost, for the poor, and for those who could not or would not hope. He came to uplift humanity, to conserve spiritual resources, and to direct all of life. He is a friend of all those who have failed and fallen.

Where, then, do we look for Him now? Among the outcasts are: those in prisons and homes for the aged, those who hunger after truth and those who are hungry, and those who dwell in darkness. This Man receiveth sinners; He is in their midst bringing new power and hope.

THIS MAN DOETH MANY MIRACLES

According to the records found in John 11:47, a council of high priests and Pharisees had been hurriedly convened; the reason for their meeting was to discuss the raising of Lazarus from the dead. Through the miracles, the group felt many persons might believe Jesus and follow Him, thus bringing in the Roman authorities. It was the advice of Caiphas that it would be expedient if one man died to save the whole nation.

These enemies of Jesus clearly understood the importance of His miracles as signs of His coming Kingdom. His enemies proclaimed His miracles and witnessed to their power over human beings.

In the stories of lepers cleansed, of devils dispossessed, of tempests stilled, of the hungry fed, of paralytics vitalized, and of the dead raised up, His enemies understood what the Kingdom would mean: a return to God's law, which is what troubled them greatly for it meant their dismissal.

NEVER MAN [SO] SPAKE

The men who first uttered these words were officers sent to arrest Jesus. They were emissaries of the enemies of Jesus. They were, if not hostile, certainly impartial.

At the time of their arrival, Jesus was exercising His public ministry in Jerusalem and was the center of criticism and discussion. The religious rulers had already decided what to do with Him; for this reason, they sent officers to arrest Him.

Three lines of meditation can be followed in understanding what the officers meant by saying, "... Never man spake like this man." First, we need to examine the content of His speech. Second, we should compare this with other forms of speech. Third, we should investigate the speaker Himself.

It would be too long of a study to consider all His words, though an examination of some of His speaking would bring us face to face with His authority. Think of just one of His sayings: "Heaven and earth shall pass away, but my words shall not pass away." (Matthew 24:35)

In the context of our present meditation, it is important to confine our attention to His speech as the officers listened to Him. During the Feast of the Tabernacles in Jerusalem, when people were astounded by His teaching, He had responded: "... My doctrine is not mine, but his that sent me." The people were deeply moved and wondered if the rulers understood that Jesus was the Christ. Jesus had responded: "... I am not come of myself, but he that sent me is true, whom ye know not. But I know him: for I am from him, and he hath sent me." It was here that the rulers decided to arrest Him.

"... Yet a little while I am with you, and *then* I go unto him that sent me. Ye shall seek me, and shall not find *me*: and where I am, *thither* ye cannot come." These words are the response of Jesus to the rulers. They could not touch Him; He was under higher authority. Nothing in world literature compares to this declaration.

We now come to the inevitable question: Who is Jesus? The officers and their rulers came face to face with this question but rejected it out of hardness of heart or fear. This Man shows the voice of God speaking in human form and in history. Never mere man so spake.

WE KNOW THAT THOU ART TRUE

Tuesday of Holy Week was the day of great controversy and questions, when Jesus was in the temple teaching. He had spoken three parables, one of which had the religious rulers passing sentence on themselves.

Those who questioned Jesus were "disciples of the Pharisees," but not the Pharisees themselves for they had been answered previously. Their question was: "... Is it lawful to give tribute unto Caesar, or not?" The religious rulers had turned to the method which was despicable, laying traps for Him. With some degree of civility, however, these disciples of the Pharisees came to Him with these words:

1. "... we know that thou art true, ..." This refers to His character.
2. "... teachest the way of God in truth, ..." This refers to His public teaching.
3. "... neither carest thou for any *man*: ..." This affirms His lack of regard for man-made barriers.
4. "... thou regardest not the person of men." This affirms His disregard for social position.

While these words were malicious and without sincere meaning, in saying them, the enemies of Jesus revealed His glory. That they were insincere is proven by the sharp answer they received from Jesus: "... Why tempt ye me, ye hypocrites?" He saw through their mask of sincerity and tore it off. Yet their words attest to His power.

In saying "... we know that thou art true, ..." His enemies paid tribute to the moral perfection of Jesus. His foes could not find fault in Him; His behavior harmonized with His teachings. He Himself was the Gospel. He taught the way of God in truth. He did not change His teaching to fit the occasion or the person. He is God's full and final word to the world.

HE SAVED OTHERS; HIMSELF HE CANNOT SAVE

These words were uttered by religious rulers in Israel, the chief priests. The words were spoken among themselves but evidently in the hearing of the assembled people around the cross.

The words were spoken with directness and mockery. They were words of jeering contempt. "... If he be the King of Israel, let him now come down from the cross, and we will believe him."

"He saved others; ..."—this was a fact they could not deny. Everywhere around them were persons who had been saved. Palsied limbs were stilled with peacefulness. Blind eyes were made to see. Persons oppressed with disease were set free. The dead were raised again.

Let us look at Him as they saw Him. It was the hour when Jesus had been lifted up on His cross between two thieves. Two ugly words cover the whole scene: condemned and executed. The rulers had plotted His death; now as they watched His painful death, they must have felt rid of Him finally. He is silent and unable to save Himself—or so they must have imagined.

Consider their double mistake. He well could have saved Himself, perhaps by bargaining with Pilate, appealing to the crowd, or even calling on God to help. He could have saved Himself but not by a show of strength—not with their methods.

He could not save Himself because He would not. This was the fact His enemies could not understand; this was their double mistake. He was cooperating with God, destroying the final hold of death on God's will. He accepted the cross in order to insure the salvation inspired by divine love.

In the mouths of His enemies, we have the greatest testimony of God's will. He could not save Himself because He was determined to save others. Such a loving Being loved us to the end and with that love reestablished our relationship to the Father.

CHAPTER

XI
MEDITATIONS ON JESUS
AND OUR LIVES TODAY

(Editor's Note: Dr. Morgan made a daily practice of reading and study-
ing the Bible. From these regular meditations he developed short sermons or interpretations, meant to be used by others in their day-to-day
Bible readings. Many of these short interpretations were given as radio
messages over a three-year period in Philadelphia. The reader might do
well to follow Dr. Morgan's pattern of Biblical study, perhaps reading the
Scripture cited before reading his comments.)

THE BAPTISM OF JESUS (Luke 3:21, 22)

There is no doubt that one of the most important acts of preparation for His public ministry was this hour when Jesus came to the River
Jordan and was baptized by John. It must have been a moving moment
for John, too, for he knew that this man was the Son of God.

In Luke's story of the life of Jesus, it strikes John the Baptist that he
should be baptized by Jesus. Why, then, did Jesus come to John? Surely,
first of all, it was because this act was His public dedication to the will of
God. And again, in this act He identified Himself with the oppressed and
suffering of the world. Though there was no need for Him to be baptized,
He humbled Himself and confessed His need of God.

Look, too, at the two verses closely, especially concerning the attitude
of Jesus. Luke says "... [he was] praying, ..." as was to be the case before all
the great events in His life: before He elected His Disciples, before His
arrest, and even on the cross itself. Again, Luke says "... the heaven was
opened, ..." and there came the outward manifestation of the Holy Spirit.
What does this mean? One theologian has suggested that the descending
dove in the account had a twofold significance. First of all, the dove signified the humility and gentleness of Jesus. Secondly, the dove signified the
sacrifice of Jesus for the sake of the world.

Then came the voice out of Heaven: "... in thee I am well pleased."
Perhaps this did not simply mean approval of His first thirty years, but also
of the meaning of His remaining three-and-a-half years to come.

The message of these verses for us today is, first of all, to marvel at His public confession of God. So, too, we who are His followers should confess Him. So may His Holy Spirit descend upon our lives to give us comfort, guidance, and courage.

JESUS CALLS LEVI (Luke 5:27, 28, 32)

There is no more fascinating form of Bible study than that of watching Jesus in His dealings with individuals. He never used the same approach with any two persons, but recognized the uniqueness of each individual. Such is the case with Levi, whom most scholars believe was Matthew.

Consider the character of Matthew. He was a Hebrew interested in government; we encounter him collecting the toll—a tax gathered for Rome. His business would make him despised by his fellow countrymen. After the call from Jesus, moreover, it can be seen that Matthew was a man of action, for he wanted his friends to know Jesus.

It is important also to notice the method of Jesus as He called Matthew. Luke says that Jesus beheld Matthew and said to him, " .. Follow me." This must have happened quickly, but it was an invitation, almost a command.

The Pharisees criticized Jesus for His call of Matthew. They could not understand how He could so closely associate with tax collectors and other sinners. Jesus' response was direct: "I came not to call the righteous, but sinners to repentance." He admitted their charge but turned it around to show He had come to restore the lost to God.

To all who are lost and oppressed, Jesus commands: Follow me. Trust me. Accept me. Join me in my way

A SCRIPTURAL MINISTRY (Luke 4:16-21)

This passage records the first remembered sermon that Jesus preached in the synagogue at Nazareth, although He certainly made it His custom to enter the synagogue on the Sabbath. The passage of Scripture that Jesus read that day was from the Book of Isaiah concerning the Servant of God who was to come, the One who said, "The Spirit of the Lord *is* upon me, ..." The program which followed from this declaration was that He had been appointed to preach good tidings to the poor, to proclaim release to the captives, to help the blind regain their sight, to set free those who were bruised, and to proclaim the acceptable year of the Lord.

Luke says that when Jesus finished reading the lesson, He sat down, adopting the attitude of the public teacher. "... This day," He said, "is this scripture fulfilled in your ears." All those who heard were amazed at His teaching, since they had known this person as the son of a mere carpenter.

There are two major lessons from this brief account. First, Jesus believed in the teachings of the Old Testament; in them He discovered

God's purposes. Second, in His reading of Isaiah, Jesus set before us the mission of the Christian community for all time: to preach glad tidings to the poor, proclaim release to the captives, help the blind receive their sight, set free those who are bruised, and proclaim the acceptable year of the Lord.

JESUS INSISTS ON RIGHTEOUSNESS (Luke 6:39-45)

In the words of Jesus recorded in Luke, there are three parables or figures of speech through which He teaches the importance of righteousness. These three figures of speech are: the blind leading the blind, the beam and mote in the eye, and a tree and its fruit.

Jesus begins with a question: Can the blind lead the blind? In Verse 40, He explains what is meant. If our living is not righteous, how can we guide others? Next, He asks how it is possible for someone with a beam in his eye to remove the mote in a brother's eye. In other words, how can we call others to righteousness if we ourselves are not righteous? Finally, He presents the picture of a good tree bringing forth good fruit and a corrupt tree bearing corrupt fruit. If our lives are not in harmony with the will of God, our impact on others will not lead them to the Gospel.

In order to have the fruit of righteousness in human relationships, we must first have the root of a right relationship to God. This is an eternal law which we cannot escape. Our world, our nation, and our lives must be right with God before we can expect righteousness. But more than this, if our personal lives are right with God, there will be the fruit of right relationships with others.

JESUS ANSWERS A DOUBTER (Luke 7:19-28)

In these passages, we have the words sent by John the Baptist to Jesus: "... Art thou he that should come? Or look we for another?" These were the words of someone who was perplexed and expected the Messiah to announce and build a visible Kingdom.

How did Jesus answer John? He did not charge John with disloyalty nor judge him for an honest question. His answer was direct: "... Go your way, and tell John what things ye have seen and heard; how that the blind see, the lame walk, the lepers are cleansed, the deaf hear, the dead are raised, to the poor the gospel is preached."

The great ministry of the Messiah had begun. It was a ministry of alleviating suffering, sin, and sorrow. Jesus did not talk about an armed insurrection, but rather about doing good. He did not talk about violence, but rather about the defeat of death. He did not talk about economic redistribution of wealth, but rather about the true wealth of being restored to God's purpose.

Many of us today are similar to John the Baptist. Because we see no visible campaign, we think the Gospel is dead. We do not pause to see the alleviation of suffering carried on in His name by followers everywhere. We do not stop to consider the victory over the forces of death and destruction which can be ours. To such persons, Jesus answers again: I am in your midst, overcoming suffering, sin, and sorrow.

JESUS IN PRAYER (Luke 9:28-36)

This passage records one of the great moments in His life: the hour of Transfiguration. Matthew, Mark, and Luke record this event in some detail and all place it at the same time in His ministry.

Luke gives special attention to the record. First, notice the time as indicated in Verse 28, "... eight days after these sayings, ..." After what sayings? If we look back to the preceding verses, we see that the sayings were when Jesus had first spoken plainly to His Disciples about the necessity of the cross. The impact of His announcement had stunned them. During the interval of days afterwards, there is no record of what happened; perhaps the Disciples retreated into despair and disbelief. But eight days later, there occurs the mighty revelation of His majesty.

As Jesus was praying, He was transfigured before them. While they were still silent and bewildered, Jesus communicated with God through prayer. He went into solitude to the loneliness of the mountain. Yet He was not really alone; He was in the presence of God. And Luke continues, "... as he prayed, the fashion of his countenance was altered, and his raiment was white *and* glistening."

What happened at this transfiguration scene?

G. Campbell Morgan said it was not a light falling on Him from Heaven nor the presence of God showing outwardly, but rather that He came to the natural end of His human life. He could have chosen eternity, then, but rather turned His face toward Jerusalem, accepting fully God's plan of salvation. He translated vision into action.

In our prayers, too, we must become enlightened by the presence of God. We should not remain with the vision or retreat into "spiritualism," but rather turn our faces back to the world, going down into the valley of darkness to bring the light of the Gospel.

JESUS TEACHES NEIGHBORLINESS (Luke 10:25-37)

The story of the Good Samaritan is well known and often quoted. What is true of all the parables is especially true of this one: It is true in terms of human experience, has an absolute simplicity, and has an abiding quality.

The parable was addressed to answer the question: Who is my neighbor? Luke writes that a certain lawyer stood up to tempt Him with the question. In response, Jesus told the parable. The story begins with the phrase, "... a certain lawyer ..." No mention is made of race or religion. The point of the story is that the Samaritan helped; he did not ask about race or religion, but simply responded to human need. He exemplified the love of neighbor which is the heart of the Gospel. To inherit eternal life is first and always to love God and the neighbor.

What does this parable mean for us today? First, the good neighbor was sensitive to the distress of others. He was not slow to respond. Second, he rendered personal service; he bound up the wounds and brought him to an inn. Third, that being a good neighbor rose out of the love of God in the man's heart. It is only when we find God as Father that we see our neighbor as brothers and sisters.

JESUS TEACHES HIS DISCIPLES TO PRAY (Luke 11:1-13)

Luke is the Gospel of the prayers of Jesus. How repeatedly it is written "He went aside to pray" or "as He was praying." It is not unusual that His Disciples asked Jesus how to pray, remembering that John the Baptist's disciples asked him the same question.

In response to His Disciples, Jesus taught them with what has traditionally been called "the Lord's Prayer," or the great pattern prayer. It is important to notice how the prayer proceeds. It commences with the prayer of passion for the Father's will and Kingdom to prevail. This first petition is not for ourselves, but for the Kingdom. The second petition is for daily sustenance, remembering the pronouns used are "our," "us," and "my" or "me." The petition is not one of selfish preservation, but brotherly concern. The third petition is for forgiveness, but one based on our forgiveness of others. The final petition is for freedom from temptation.

In the third through thirteenth verses of Luke, we find the pictures which Jesus used to illustrate the naturalness and glory of prayer.

One of the first pictures is of a friend at midnight who is in need of extra food to feed unexpected guests. Because the friend continues to knock at the door, the parable concludes that his request will be met. The second picture is that of the loving father who gives gifts to his children. How much more, then, will the Heavenly Father not give good gifts to His children?

The key words in these pictures are: how much more. If a man will answer a friend at midnight, how much more will God not respond to

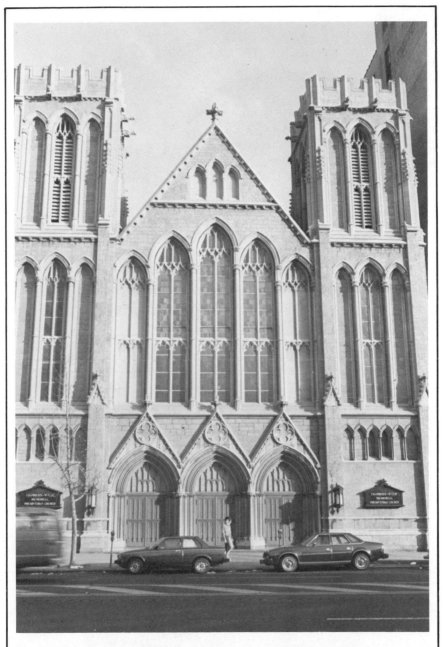

The Chambers-Wylie Memorial Presbyterian Church, Philadelphia, where Dr. Morgan spent 26 years as senior minister and, then, became Minister Emeritus in 1976.

In 1957, Howard Moody Morgan and his sons (left to right) Howard, John, and Richard.

Grandparents, Margaret and Howard, with infant Pam, 1959.

Howard and 18-month-old granddaughter Pam, 1960.

Family reunion, 1965, (left to right): Mary Ann, daughter; Howard Moody Morgan; Margaret, wife; and his other children—Howard, Patricia, Richard, and John.

Howard Moody Morgan and ninth grandchild Jennifer Lee, 1966.

Howard Moody Morgan, 1968.

those who ask? Or again, if a father will provide for a child, how much more will God not provide for us?

Jesus teaches His Disciples to ask, seek, and knock. These words suggest urgent and persistent intercession. Prayer is an active relationship and a petition that will be answered if requested earnestly and in faith.

JESUS EXPLAINS THE KINGDOM (Luke 13:18-30)

In Verses 18 through 21, there are two brief parables that Jesus uses to describe the Kingdom of God. There are often two interpretations of these parables, the most common being that Jesus wanted to show how from small beginnings the Kingdom grows into greater power. Another, less held view is that the teaching is a warning that the Kingdom is not meant to be a material event, but rather inward and spiritual.

In Verse 23, someone asked Jesus, "... Lord, are there few that be saved?" Jesus did not give a dogmatic response, but rather a direct one: "Strive to enter in at the strait gate: ..." What He really said was: Don't waste your time with such questions; look to yourself.

Jesus also said that mere familiarity with Him does not guarantee entrance into the Kingdom. Neither does blood relationship or adherence to certain religious teachings guarantee entrance. Rather, the Kingdom grows from personal relationship to Him and the Father.

THE GOSPEL FOR ALL (Luke 14:12-24)

These verses contain the parable of a certain man who made a great supper and invited many people. It is, of course, a picture of God Himself in Christ making ready in His loving provision for all those who accept His mercy. But the story goes on to tell how those who had been invited made excuses so they would not have to attend the feast.

In this parable, we are given the story of the love of God for all people and also the foolishness of persons who do not accept the invitation.

In previous verses of the fourteenth chapter, we are given pictures of the kinds of persons who will not enter the Kingdom. They are self-notioned; they believe they already possess the truth. They also are self-exalted people, feeling themselves better than others. They are finally self-excusing individuals, finding any way out of accepting the invitations. Remember what kind of excuses they gave: attention to business, pride of possession, and fear of consequences.

The message of this parable is that Jesus invites all people into His Kingdom. His call is for the life of the self-emptying Disciple who does the will of God.

JESUS AND HUMAN WORTH (Luke 8: 26-37)

The world has become so mechanical that we are in danger of becoming victims of our own technology. We even end measuring a person's worth by how much is owned or how much accomplished. Yet, Jesus blessed no person for what had been done or accumulated, but rather for the quality of humanity and spirituality evident. Think of the Beatitudes; they all relate to blessings on people and on the quality and depth of their lives.

In Luke 8:26-37, we find three worlds meeting: the underworld of evil spirits, the world of human experience, and the world of divine love in Christ. Luke describes the world of evil spirits in terms of the man in the story, who "... ware no clothes, neither abode in *any* house, but in the tombs." This is the picture of a person possessed by some demon, some force beyond his control.

When Jesus comes his way, His divine power is recognized by the man: "... What have I to do with thee, Jesus, *thou* Son of God most high?" But Jesus relates the person within: "What is thy name?" He calls the man back to reality and sanity. There follows the command of Jesus that the demons should enter into the herd of swine feeding nearby, and they rush down the steep into the sea.

Upon being healed, the man fled into the city and told all. In telling all, there were probably some who criticized Jesus for destroying the swine. We must remember that in all the New Testament only here and in the story where Jesus withered the fig tree is there any record of Jesus bringing destruction. But Jesus saw infinite significance and dignity in human life. Those who criticized Him often put more stock in their property than they did in human life. It is the solemn duty of all those who call themselves His Disciples to proclaim the absolute dignity of human life, against all those who place property or profits first.

JESUS TEACHES FORGIVENESS (John 8:2-11)

The teaching of Jesus about forgiveness takes place when the unforgiving Pharisees bring into the Temple a woman who they have caught in the act of sin. They make a public scene in order to test Jesus, thus manipulating the woman in the process. They did not bring her out of love or righteousness, but rather to catch Jesus.

If Jesus acquitted the woman, He would be breaking the law of Moses. If He condemned the woman, He would have been encroaching upon the authority of Rome. To the accusers, He said nothing at first. He stooped and wrote on the ground; we do not know what He wrote. Some have suggested He wrote the words that He was about to utter: "... He that is without sin among you, let him first cast a stone at her." Others have suggested He wrote the name of some sin in the lives of the accusers so that they might know the wickedness of their own lives. Perhaps He wrote only because of the shame He felt for this woman.

When Jesus said, "... He that is without sin among you, let him first cast a stone ... ," the accusers dropped their stones. In all the relationships of life, from the personal to the social, these words ought to be written in fire, so others are not judged so harshly. G. Campbell Morgan once said that he only heard one man who had the right to preach about Hell: D. L. Moody. He said so because Moody never spoke about Hell without tears in his eyes. If judgment is to be passed, it must be done out of compassion.

As the story concludes, the poor woman is left alone with Jesus. Jesus asks her: "... Woman, where are those thine accusers? ..." Seeing none, He forgives her. He accepted her repentance and charged her to begin a new life.

The message here for us is to possess the forgiving spirit. Before we judge or condemn anyone, we should pause and remember that we all are sinners. Then, if judgment must be pronounced, it will be done in loving tenderness and not bitterness.

THE DANGERS OF RICHES (Luke 16:19-31)

These verses are often called the Parable of Dives and the Poor Beggar. They present the teachings of Jesus about possessions. There are some who would say Jesus had nothing to say about poverty or wealth, but only about the Gospel. But what Gospel? Surely the Gospel is both love of God and love of neighbor, and surely the neighbor is someone in need whether that need be emotional or economic. Jesus did look at the real neighbor, and we cannot escape our obligation to do likewise.

The parable sketches out a drama in two scenes. The first scene is on earth. A rich man is seen, clothed in fine linen, faring very well. However, it is not his riches which are at issue, but rather his lack of sympathy for those who have little. The second scene is in Heaven. In painting this picture, Jesus says, "... the beggar died, ..." The rich man also dies. The parable conveys the message of Jesus that those who trust material possessions, and do not use their wealth for others, are in danger.

The whole parable is a warning about self-indulgence and abuse of our blessings. To be Christlike, it is necessary that we share whatever possessions we have with others, just as He shared Himself with us.

JESUS INSPIRES HONESTY (Luke 19:1-10)

The account of Zaccheus is a thrilling story of how Jesus changed one man from being mastered by selfishness and greed into being a new man in Christ. Jesus inspires us to be honest.

Jesus was passing through Jericho when He encountered a man named Zaccheus, whom Luke tells us was "... chief among the publicans, and he was rich." We know that the publicans were tax gatherers, and we also know that to be rich they probably did not give Rome all the taxes due. One historian says that in one town in Palestine a monument was erected to one publican because he was known to be honest!

Zaccheus was probably a dishonest man. When Jesus came near him, He told Zaccheus that He needed to stay at his house. What happened during His stay we do not know, but we do know that Zaccheus became a new man. "... Behold, Lord, the half of my goods I give to the poor; and if I have taken any thing from any man by false accusation, I restore *him* fourfold." The final words of Jesus on this occasion are striking: "... This day is salvation come to this house, ... For the Son of man is come to seek and to save that which was lost."

There are two tremendously important truths in this teaching. First, Jesus said the reason Zaccheus became honest was that salvation had come. In other words, the change had to come internally, from some basic transformation of the self. Second, Jesus said He came to save the lost, not only from God but also lost from just relationships with others.

Being honest to God means being open to the power of Jesus and, then, acting upon this new being with justice and love.

THE FRIEND OF SINNERS (Luke 7:36-50)

Jesus was invited to dinner in the house of a Pharisee named Simon. We do not know why Simon invited Jesus, but in all probability he was curious about His teachings. During the course of the dinner an invited woman, possibly someone whom Jesus had forgiven earlier, came into the room to pour out her alabaster box of ointment in thankfulness. Here is the record of one sinner who found salvation.

But there is another person in this story who needed the forgiveness of Jesus: Simon, the proud Pharisee. It is important to note how Luke portrays Simon. When he first sees the woman approaching Jesus, he begins to "... spake within himself, ..." One can well imagine him thinking that Jesus was no prophet at all if He allowed this sinning woman to touch Him.

In telling Simon the parable of the two debtors, Jesus revealed to him his own need for forgiveness.

The first lesson from this parable is that Jesus meets the needs of all classes and conditions of persons. Whether it be the poor woman or the rich Pharisee, forgiveness is necessary. Second, there is a clear relationship between forgiveness and loving devotion. When someone is truly forgiven, there is a response of abandoned devotion. Jesus welcomes this devotion and love.

THE SCOURGED CHRIST (Matthew 27:26-31)

All the considerations of Jesus lead to the cross, for here is the heart of the Gospel. All four Gospel writers present the story surrounding His death, giving importance to the meaning of the atoning death. Jesus Himself often said to His Disciples, "... mine hour is not yet come." and then on the night of His betrayal said, "the hour is come; ..."

Think for a minute of those verses described by Matthew which tell of His scourging before they marched Him out from the hall to the hill called Calvary. We can gain three pictures from reading the Scripture. First, consider Pilate, who delivered Jesus up to be crucified. Pilate refused to use his high office to save Him, even though he knew Him to be innocent. He put policy above principle.

The second picture is that of the poor deluded soldiers, mocking and jeering Jesus. They put a crown of thorns on His head, spit upon Him, and smote Him. And, perhaps the greatest sin, they put a military robe on Him, this Servant of God, the Prince of Peace. Even then, Jesus forgave them.

The third and final picture is that of Jesus Himself, infinitely patient and loving, even unto death and suffering. The only answer He gave was to arise from this scene of insult and take up His cross in perfect obedience to the will of God. God, through Jesus, loves us, even unto death.

JESUS EXALTED (Matthew 28:1-10)

Jesus never spoke of His cross without speaking of the Resurrection. Remember how He taught His Disciples, "... the Son of man must suffer many things, and be rejected of the elders, and of the chief priests, and scribes, and be killed, and after three days rise again."

Matthew recalls the events leading up to the cross and Resurrection. It was dawn at the tomb, where His body had been lain. When the women came to the place where He was buried, the stone had been rolled away and they encountered an angel who said "... he is risen, as he said." And then followed a command to these women to be the first heralds of the Risen Lord. And Jesus appeared to the women, saying: "... Be not afraid: go tell my brethren ... shall they see me."

It should be noted that both the angel and Jesus used the same words as the Resurrection greeting: "... Fear not ..." Surely this is the heart of the message. The fear of death is often with us. Most lives are under the shadow of some great fear. But Jesus offers hope. By some great mystery He comes into our lives to set us free from fear. Thus, we say Jesus is alive and exalted.

There are three great meanings of this story recorded by Matthew. First, the Resurrection is the ground of hope and the rock of faith. His resurrection also provides the power for holy living. If the tomb had held Him, then evil would have been the victor. But He rose, calling us all to overcome evil in His name. And finally, His resurrection is the pledge of eternal life. Death is not the end of our pilgrimage, for Jesus has shown that not even death can separate us from the love of God which was in Christ Jesus.

POSTSCRIPT

HOWARD MOODY MORGAN: PASTORAL PREACHER

When I behold the sacred *liao wo* my thoughts return to those who begot me, raised me, and now are tired. I would repay the bounty they have given me; But it is as the sky; it can never be approached.

In 1857, Anthony Trollope wrote in the *Barchester Towers*, "There is, perhaps, no greater hardship at present inflicted on mankind in civilized and free countries, than the necessity of listening to sermons." Such was never the case for those who listened to the sermons of Howard Moody Morgan. Steeped in the rich tradition of English expository preaching, especially as articulated by G. Campbell Morgan, his father and teacher, Dr. Morgan brought the Word of God to people in an unforgettable manner.

The sermons in this volume, *The God-Man of Galilee*, reflect Dr. Morgan's creative synthesis of British expository preaching (his spiritual roots) and American pastoral preaching (his developed style). While Dr. Morgan would be the first to acknowledge his debt to the expository preaching of his father, only now, we of another generation recognize the uniqueness of these sermons.

Dr. Morgan was first and foremost a biblical preacher, a man of the Word. He stood in the tradition of British expository preaching, which his father, G. Campbell Morgan of London, made so powerful in the twentieth century. In his book on preaching, Campbell Morgan wrote,

The supreme work of the Christian minister is the work of preaching. This is a day in which one of our great perils is that of doing a thousand little things to the neglect of one thing, which is preaching.[1]

Preaching, according to Campbell Morgan, was proclaiming the Good News and that suggested two things: the need of man and the grace of

God. "Whenever we preach we stand between these two things: between human need and Divine Grace. We are messengers of that grace to human need."[2] For two years, Howard Moody Morgan traveled with his father and studied for the ministry under his direct supervision. In the fifteenth annual Campbell Morgan Memorial Lecture of 1963, Dr. Morgan acknowledged his debt to his "goodly heritage."

> Campbell Morgan was the father of my flesh, but also, and more so, under the power of the Holy Spirit, the father of my spiritual life. My congregations in five churches in the United States and England have heard me say many times, 'As my father and teacher said or wrote.'[3]

Preaching the Word meant long, painstaking hours of preparation by study of the Scriptures. In commenting on the work of the preacher, Campbell Morgan said,

> That is the supreme work of the Christian minister and preacher. He is set free from the secular calling of life so that he may consecrate his time to these sacred Writings, and work all the week at them, in order that when his people gather he may guide them and lead them into the sacred truths of the sacred Book. Any man in the ministry who is frittering away his time on a hundred trifles, and neglects the hard working, sweating preparation for his pulpit is a renegade to his calling.[4]

Dr. Morgan often recalled with amusement an incident which occurred in one of his churches. A Presbyterian deacon asked his youngest son, John, if he were going to be a preacher like his grandfathers, uncles, father, and brother, and John replied, "Nope! I'm going to work." Little did he realize that there were long hours of painstaking study of the Scriptures which lay behind his father's sermons. Dr. Morgan believed in spending an hour in preparation for every minute he stood in the pulpit preaching. A strange irony of history took place when this youngest son entered the parish ministry 30 years later and began the *work* of the ministry. Dr. Morgan was "... a workman that needeth not to be ashamed, rightly dividing the word of truth." (II Timothy 2:15) What characterized his sermons was his declaring the *whole* counsel of God (Acts 20:27). His sermons were always couched in the language of the Bible. As he had learned from his father, "Never handle the text, let the text handle you." He made the Word of God living and active and sharper than any two-edged sword (Hebrews 4:12).

   Dr. Morgan's own view of preaching was clearly set forth in his lecture, "The Word of God Through the Words of Men,"

> If ever the pulpit becomes the mere platform for a man's eloquence, or as a sounding board for a man to launch his commentaries on current events, then indeed can be written across that pulpit, 'Ichabod'—for the glory hath departed. If the pulpit becomes the rostrum for the perpetuation of pet theological obsessions with undue emphasis upon one doctrine while failing to proclaim the whole counsel of God, then indeed the total glory of the Word is under eclipse.[5]

Because he had spent precious hours with the prophets of Israel, he could speak with prophetic passion to the issues of his day: racism, sexism, and nationalism. Having steeped himself in the words and mind of Christ in the Gospels, he could bring that same message to people in urban America. Once, he told his oldest son, Richard, that one of his favorite quotations came from *The Imitation of Christ* by Thomas A'Kempis. "He to whom the Eternal Word speaks, is delivered from a multitude of opinions." In a century when theological opinions and endless controversy over doctrinal issues permeated the American pulpits, this servant of the Lord spoke an eternal Word because he had heard that word in the Bible. His sermons remind us of what Charles E. Jefferson said of preaching, "Drops of blood shed by the servants of the Lord for the redemption of the world."

Howard Moody Morgan was a *pastoral preacher*. Unlike his brother, Dr. F. Crossley Morgan, who spent most of his ministry as an itinerant Bible teacher, Dr. Morgan's preaching grew out of his work as a pastor. Here, again, he perpetuated the model of his father, G. Campbell Morgan, who had served nine parishes in England and America and whose preaching had grown out of his love of people. As Dr. Morgan said of his own father, "While he was always the preacher to the great crowds, he had an infinitely lovely personal touch with people, those the world would call 'the lowly and little people.' "[6] In the Sprunt Lectures of 1919 at Union Theological Seminary in Richmond, Virginia, Campbell Morgan described this pastoral aspect of preaching in this manner,

> The Pastor-Teacher has more to do than preach to his congregation...'Every man' is never reached in general teaching. The Pastor-Teacher must acquaint himself with the individuals which make up his flock. He must get to know them personally. Every man has his own idiosyncrasy, peculiarity, problem, temptation, capacity.[7]

As a pastor for more than 55 years, Dr. Morgan knew the needs of his people by constant pastoral contact. In a striking fashion, Dr. Morgan's ministry in Philadelphia paralleled the pastoral preaching of Dr. Harry

Emerson Fosdick in New York. Fosdick believed that "Every sermon should have for its main business the solution of some problem, a vital, important problem, puzzling minds, bothering consciences, distracting lives."[8] Dr. Morgan, who often quoted Fosdick, focused his sermons on the needs of people. The series of sermons in this volume, "Answers of Christ to the Questions of Man," "The Power of Christ for Human Problems," and "Eternal Answers to Modern Questions" reflect this pastoral preaching. As a pastor, he had listened to the fears and anxieties of those who faced major life crises; he had sat by the bedside of the aged and dying; he had borne the burden with those who had suffered tragedies; and he had ministered to those who experienced the gnawing hopelessness of poverty and unemployment. As Martin Luther said, "God hides himself in the neighbor," so Dr. Morgan found God in the agonies and anguish of humanity.

He had a special ministry to the outsiders. He used to love to tell the story of the little boy who was asked by his Sunday School teacher why the priest and Levite passed up the man who had been robbed, and the lad answered, "Because they saw he had already been robbed!" Dr. Morgan would then chide the church for ignoring those who had nothing to offer the church in wealth or position. His social gospel becomes abundantly clear in his sermon, "This Man Receiveth Sinners" from Luke 15:2, "Where, then, do we look for him now? Among the outcasts, those in prisons and homes for the aged; those who hunger after truth and are hungry, those who dwell in darkness ... He is friend of all who have failed and fallen."

He had a special ministry to children and the aged. At the ordination service of his oldest son, Richard, in 1953, Dr. Morgan quoted the words of John G. Whittier's hymn, *Immortal Love:*

> Through him the first fond prayers are said
> Our lips of childhood frame
> The last low whispers of our dead
> Are burdened with his name.
>
> (John G. Whittier, 1886)

These words reflect his own unique ministry to the young and the old. He was the idol of children, who loved his funny stories, clown-like antics, impromptu songs at the piano, and the way he would wriggle his upper lip like a rabbit. He always wore the British clerics, and once, while walking down a city street in Philadelphia, a man mistook him for a Catholic priest and said, "Good morning, father." Dr. Morgan replied, "Yes, I am the father of five children." But like Joseph, who became the foster-father of our Lord, Dr. Morgan became the foster-father of many children and touched their lives with love and kindness. He loved to visit the "shut-ins" and aged of his congregation and community. Despite his disdain for the term "senior citizen," he literally tramped hundreds of miles across the city of Philadelphia visiting the aged and conducting services in Homes for the Aged. His youngest son, John, wrote of him,

> He talked about himself as 'a patriarch,' and 'the old man,' but somehow he never acted the role of a 'senior citizen.' He never went to a senior center. He didn't plan very well financially for his retirement. He always seemed uneasy taking social security checks.[9]

But he had a special concern for the aged, for "those who sit in darkness and the shadow of death." He, who would not "go gentle into that good night," spent many an hour with the dying, ministering to them with faith and love. The pastoral ministry of Howard Moody Morgan reminds one of the words of Chaucer about the good parson in the Canterbury Tales.

> The word of Christ most truly did he preach
> And his parishioners devoutly teach
> Benign was he—in labours diligent
> And in adversity was still content—
> As proved full oft. To all his flock a friend—
> Wide was his parish, scattered far asunder
> Yet none did he neglect, in rain or thunder.
> Sorrow and sickness won his kindly care;
> With staff in hand he travelled everywhere.
> ... The lore of Christ and his apostles twelve,
> He taught, but first he followed it himself.[10]

Reading the sermons of Howard Moody Morgan makes one realize that they reflect his own discipleship of the God-Man of Galilee. Henri Nouwen has said that "Preaching should be a way of relating to men and women so that they are able to respond to what is said with their own life-experience."[11] Preaching becomes real when people find a sounding board in their own personal experience. Because Howard Moody Morgan lived life to its fullest, his words found an anchor place in the lives of his hearers. He broke the stereotype of the "professional cleric," despite his clerical garb. He was unashamedly human, and this became a bridge between him and his hearers. When he learned that the librarian at Union Theological Seminary in Richmond, Virginia had mistakenly cataloged the life of his father as "A Man of the *World*" instead of "A Man of the Word," he chuckled and said: "Well, he was that, too." And so was Howard Moody Morgan, whose earthiness and unabashed involvement in life fleshed out the Word in his own experience. As Nouwen has said,

> Pastoral care means in the final analysis: Offering your life-experience to your fellowman and as Paul Simon sings, to lay yourself down like a bridge over troubled waters.[12]

When people listened to Dr. Morgan, they knew they heard a man who was available to himself and, therefore, able to offer his experience to others.

In 1952, he sent the following suggestions for ministry to his oldest son, Richard, who was then a senior in the seminary. They became his own summary of his ministry:

> 1. Under God, have care for your own soul. Keep bright in your devotional life, and 'maintain the spiritual glow.' To fail in this priority for Christ's minister is to fall down everywhere else.
>
> 2. With God's help, obey the old exhortation: Plan your work. Work your plan. This means *your* work and *your* plan. Do not be overwhelmed by the great ministers and their programs. Surely the secret of a Henry Ward Beecher, a Charles Haddon Spurgeon, a Ralph W. Sockman, and a George Buttrick lies in the fact they were Beecher, Spurgeon, Sockman, and Buttrick. God has given each man a talent. Be true to the gift of God in you.
>
> 3. For heaven's sake and for everybody's sake, *be human*. By all means possess dignity befitting a man of God, but radiate the gift of the Spirit—'... love, joy, peace, longsuffering, gentleness, goodness, faith, meekness, temperance: ...' And here, not to presume upon the shining sentence of the great Apostle Paul, nevertheless, I would underscore joy. The church has far too many dull, drab members and ministers, too. Above all, the chief end of man is to glorify God and enjoy Him forever.

Maintaining the spiritual glow, being true to the gift of God in him, and demonstrating a benign humanness were the unique qualities of this man.

THE ORDER OF ISAAC

In May of 1953, Dr. Morgan preached the baccalaureate sermon at the graduation services for his oldest son, Richard, at Union Theological Seminary. In this sermon he referred to himself as "belonging to the order of Isaac." "I do not believe in apostolic succession," he told the graduates, "because by the time the greatness of a father gets through to the fourth of his preacher-sons, it is an extraordinary thin stream. I feel I belong to the order of Isaac, for I have a renown father and a good son. It is great to be in the order of Isaac, blessed before and after by these men in Christ."

In a strange way, he was both right and wrong. He was an Isaac. As Isaac, or *Yitzak*, and "One who makes others laugh," he was the clerical clown whose marvelous humor became a way of contact with people. In his own vulnerability and weakness, he made contact with the clown in every man. He fulfilled the word of the ancient proverb, "A merry heart doeth good *like* a medicine: ..." (Proverbs 17:22) Like Isaac, who blessed his sons Esau and Jacob, Dr. Morgan was always blessing people with his common touch, his genuine concern, and his Christlike compassion.

Yet his humor led to communicating the Word to people along life's way. One incident Dr. Morgan recalled in his 1963 Campbell Morgan Memorial Lecture illustrated this:

> I was reading my copy of a recent edition of the New Testament on a train travelling from Philadelphia to New York where I was to attend our monthly meeting of the Board of the Bible Society. A gentleman seated by my side noticed the colourful magazine, as he thought it was, and suddenly I heard him say, 'Pardon me, but is that an abbreviated edition of "Life" which you are reading?'
>
> In the United States there is a monthly magazine called 'Life' and I could instantly understand the reason of the question. However, this was my opportunity to bear witness to the Word. I turned the book around so he could read the title, 'The New Testament of our Lord and Saviour, Jesus Christ' and then I said 'No sir, this is not an abbreviated edition of "Life" but this is THE Life'. As we journeyed on to New York, I discovered he was a Christian man and we had the joy of speaking together of our common faith.[13]

This incident was symbolic of the way Dr. Morgan's wit and humor became a bridge in communicating the Good News of God's love.

Unlike Isaac, who was merely a link between the faith of Abraham and the religious transformation of Jacob, Dr. Morgan made his own unique contribution to the religious history of his day. His preaching not only preserved the type of biblical preaching he inherited from his tradition, but the unique way he spoke to human need carved out a model of pastoral preaching which was one of a kind. His sermons, as reflected in this book, well illustrate what Charles E. Jefferson said about preaching,

> The minister must be both a good pastor and a preacher. The better he is as a pastor, the more effective he will be as a

preacher. It is because men limp and crawl in pastoral work that they often stumble and fall in the pulpit. Because they desert the people through the week, God deserts them on Sunday. A man cannot be an ideal preacher unless he has a shepherd's heart.[14]

It could never be said of Dr. Morgan that "since he was invisible during the week, he was incomprehensible on Sunday." His whole life was given as a gift of love to people whom he touched in their homes, offices, and on the common roads of life. His pastoral ministry could be summed up in the words of the poem,

> Do the work that's nearest
> Though its dull at whiles
> Helping them when we meet them
> Lame dogs over stiles;
> See in every hedgerow
> Marks of angels feet
> Epics in each pebble
> Underneath our feet.

We believe that the legacy of the sermons in this volume will continue. Although their impact is still felt by his generation, our conviction is that they will find roots in a new generation. As John C. Morgan wrote,

> Reading Dad's sermons has given me a new understanding of our common heritage. Separated by miles—and even continents—we are yet united. In spite of the problems we have encountered, we know that we were given a gift, a perspective on life, that has motivated each of us in different ways. If you remember, at the Reunion, Dad did not say he was proud of us; he said he was grateful.

We cannot but believe that in the blest communion of saints, where he in glory shines, never again to be distracted or unaware, his words live on. As G. Campbell Morgan said in his last sermon at Westminster Chapel, London, in 1945,

> That will be the essence of Heaven, to be where He is, to see Him, to hear Him, and to work for Him for He is not idle, neither are the saints that have gone, idle. They rest from their labors, but their works accompany them forth. They are still working, and we shall be.[15]

In that glorious life, where faith has become sight, and hope, reality, Howard Moody Morgan has cast his life before Him, lost in wonder, love, and praise.

> What we trust unto the dust
> Is but the earthly garb he wore;
> What we love, lives on,
> And will live forevermore.

And so, we, his children, feebly struggle to carry on his ministry, "we live to speak the Word, hear it, write it, have it, be it." Whether in the parish or the hospital, in ministry to the aged or the world of banking, our response can be no more than what Dr. Morgan often quoted at the end of his sermons,

> Saviour, dear Saviour,
> These sayings of Thine;
> Help me to make them
> Doings of mine

Patricia Ruth
Richard Lyon
Mary Ann
Howard Campbell
John Crossley

END NOTES

[1]G. Campbell Morgan, *Preaching* (Grand Rapids, Michigan: Baker Book House, 1974), p. 11.

[2]*Ibid.*, pp. 11, 12.

[3]Howard Moody Morgan, *The Word of God Through the Words of Men* (The Campbell Morgan Lectureship, July, 1963), p. 3.

[4]G. Campbell Morgan, *The Bible: 400 Years after 1538* (New York: Fleming H. Revell, 1939), p. 150.

[5]Howard Moody Morgan, p. 17.

[6]Jill Morgan, *A Man of the Word* (London: Pickering and Inglis, 1951), p. 84.

[7]G. Campbell Morgan, *The Ministry of the Word* (London: Hodder and Stoughton, 1919), p. 139.

[8]Harry Emerson Fosdick, "What Is the Matter with Preaching?" *Harpers*, July, 1928, p. 134.

[9]John Morgan, "Two Years Later: Memory of a Father," Free Press, 1981.

[10]Geoffrey Chaucer, *Canterbury Tales*, tr. H.C. Leonard.

[11]Henri Nouwen, *Creative Ministry* (New York: Image Books, 1971), p. 35.

[12]*Ibid.*, p. 38.

[13]Howard Moody Morgan, p. 13.

[14]Charles E. Jefferson, *The Minister as Shepherd* (New York: Thomas Y. Crowell, 1905), pp. 197-198.

[15]G. Campbell Morgan, *Alpha and Omega*, p. 56.

THE GOD-MAN OF GALILEE

by Howard Moody Morgan

Collected here for the first time are the selected sermons and radio addresses of Dr. Howard Moody Morgan, son of G. Campbell Morgan who was known to thousands of Christians in the United States and Great Britain as the "Prince of Biblical Expositors." Taught by his father, Howard Moody Morgan was for over five decades the preacher and pastor of Presbyterian churches and a frequent guest in English pulpits.

Dr. Morgan combined the skills of expository preaching with parish work and represented what his son Richard, himself a Presbyterian pastor, calls a "creative synthesis of British expository preaching (his spiritual roots) and American pastoral preaching (his developed style)." Compiled in this volume are sermons that span fifty years of preaching, including a prophetic series dealing with the vital role played by women in the life of the early church. Dr. Morgan advocated the ordination of women into the ministry long before it was popular.

New generations of readers can now become acquainted with the thoughts of Dr. Morgan. Readers will discover here fresh materials for Bible study and spiritual growth. As the Introduction to this book states: "Today, as when Howard Moody Morgan preached, The Word takes on flesh and meaning for our lives, if we would listen."

While the subjects will be of special interest to ministers and seminarians, the messages here will be of great interest to laypersons because the words were first addressed to persons concerned with the meaning of the Gospel in their own lives.